# WOUNDED

## How to Find Wholeness and Inner Healing in Christ

# TERRY WARDLE

### LEAFWOOD
PUBLISHERS

**WOUNDED**
*How to Find Wholeness & Inner Healing in Christ*

LEAFWOOD

Copyright © 1994, 2005 by Terry Wardle

ISBN 0-9748441-9-5    10 digit
ISBN 978-0-9748441-9-0    13 digit

Printed in the United States of America

Cover design by Rick Gibson

Leafwood Publishers is an imprint of
Abilene Christian University Press.

1626 Campus Court
Abilene, Texas 79601
1-877-816-4455 toll free

For current information about all Leafwood titles, visit our Web site:
www.leafwoodpublishers.com

11  12  13  14  /  7  6  5  4

*To my sister, Bonnie*
*Your love has been a*
*transforming presence in my life*
*for as long as I can remember*

# CONTENTS

# Introduction

I STOPPED ON THE SIDEWALK that led to the building in front of me. I could not hide or hold back my emotions any longer. As tears began to flow I turned to seek comfort and support from my wife Cheryl. She assured me of her love, God's faithfulness, and that what I was about to do was not only right, it was necessary. And then she placed her arms around me and we embraced. In all honesty I did not want to let her go!

After four months of battling deep depression, the time had come for a more aggressive approach to recovery. With her encouragement I walked through the double-glass doors leading to the Rapha Unit of Cedar Springs Psychiatric Hospital. I was admitting myself as a patient for at least twenty-one days of treatment. This was something I never thought would happen to me. But it was happening, and I had to face the fact that I needed what they could give.

Somehow, with my wife's help and the Lord's strength, I made it through all the interviews and paperwork required that day. But in more ways than one my mind wasn't focused on those standard pre-admission require-ments. Instead, I wrestled deep inside with some very important questions:

> *Is this really necessary?*
>
> *Would being in such a treatment center, even though it was Chist-centered, actually help?*
>
> *What would people think of me, a Christian leader, in need of psychiatric care?*
>
> *How did I get into this mess anyway?*
>
> *Would the pain and darkness lift as quickly as it came, or would this be a long journey through a "dark night of the soul"?*
>
> *What would this illness ultimately mean for me, my family, and my ministry?*
>
> *Where was God in all this?*

After signing the final paper, I was led down the cor-ridor to my room. Cheryl helped place my clothes in their appropriate drawers and closets. Visiting hours were over for the unit so she had to leave right away. Even though I knew she was staying in Colorado Springs in order to visit me daily, saying goodbye was very hard.

As she turned and left the room, I sat down on the edge of my bed and began to cry. It was all I could do, and in fact all I wanted to do at that moment. I felt horribly afraid, and anxious about what faced me in the days ahead. The past months had been a nightmare and that moment the worst part of the dream.

While weeping I "somehow" remembered a radio interview I had listened to some five years previous. At the time I was leading my denomination's seminary in New York. Traveling home from a speaking engagement I tuned in to a Christian radio station. The traveling companion of Corrie Ten Boom was talking about this great Christian woman's life and her impact upon the world.

She made a comment I thought profound, but really made no conscious effort to remember. In fact, until those moments on my bed it had never come to mind. But as I sat there crying, her words came back with crystal clarity. She said Miss Ten Boom had taught people that "in the hands of God, the object of one's greatest pain could become the source of one's greatest blessing."

## Prayer through Pain

Immediately I turned to God in prayer. He had been hearing from me repeatedly as I sought healing and freedom from this depression. But this time the focus of my prayer was upon the insight of Corrie Ten Boom. I told God that this was certainly the greatest trial of my life to date. And, with faith the size of a mustard seed, I offered it to Him. With sincerity and hope I committed this illness to His sovereign care, to be used however He saw fit. Admittedly I wondered if I could ever praise God for such pain and had little insight as to how this bad time could bring about any good whatsoever. Yet I closed my prayer by saying, "God, please let this season someday become a source of blessings. Amen."

It has been several years since praying on my bed at Cedar Springs Hospital. These months have included times of great pain, intense therapy, some defeats, and many victories. I am well again, but the journey has been far from easy, and in truth is not over. I have experienced the healing hand of God, times of sweet intimate communion, and hard days when He seemed silent and uninvolved. I have discovered things about myself that I never knew, or at least never faced before. Equally, there remain some unresolved issues that I trust God will address in the not-too-distant future.

But of this I am sure: God has used these events to transform my life! Like spoils after battle, my baskets are full to overflowing. I can testify without hesitation that it is true—in God's hands the object of one's greatest pain *does* become the source of one's greatest blessing!

## Key Changes

The dynamics and degrees of the Lord's work through this season of pain and recovery are far too expansive to address here. However, I will mention several key changes He has accomplished through my illness.

First and foremost, I have a much deeper understanding and experience of God's compassion for the emotionally broken. Nowhere has this been confirmed more than in the ministry of our Lord Jesus. He came not only to bear our sins but also to carry our griefs and sorrows.

Secondly, the Lord uncovered deep emotional

wounds in my life. Layer by layer He peeled away defense mechanisms and behavioral dysfunctions designed to hide past hurt and sin. Once at the core of the problem, He brought healing, deliverance, and new life to my inner being.

Thirdly, as often happens, my experience of emotional pain has been used by the Lord to sensitize me to the wounds of others. Previously, committed to hiding my own hurts, I was somewhat blinded and numbed to pain in people's lives. Today, my heart breaks for the emotionally wounded, and I ask God to use me as He so chooses to bring hope and healing in Jesus' name.

God does cause good things to come out of bad experiences. My journey to wholeness has opened the door for hundreds of people to finally admit their own pain. By being honest about my "dark night," many within my circle of influence now feel free to cry out for help. In our local church alone scores of wounded people are choosing vulnerability in order to experience the healing power of the Lord.

In addition, many believers are discovering that God can and does use counselors, therapists, and psychiatrists as agents of healing. Certainly such caregivers must be anchored in Scripture and empowered by the Holy Spirit. When they are, wounded men, women, and children can move on to emotional wholeness through their ministries.[1]

I have written this volume with one primary purpose: to offer hope to the emotionally wounded by pointing them to the Lord Jesus. His sufferings are truly central to the freedom, deliverance, and wholeness people

desperately need. Satan has victimized millions of people and the mental anguish and emotional pain are
unbearable. But in Christ there is tranformation! It is
found at the cross and is there for all who turn to Him.

## One Who Has Been There

I do not approach this book as a theologian, though
I have served as a professor for many years. Nor do I
come as a counselor, though that too has been a role I
have played in pastoral ministry. I have written this
book as one who has been there, a wounded human
being with dysfunctional behavior that ultimately led to
a breakdown. And I have written as one who has been
restored beyond expectation by the love of God, displayed through the unsearchable riches of Christ Jesus.
He has touched the deepest part of my being and
brought healing beyond description. While He used
many instruments along the way, Jesus alone has been
my Healer.

I have restricted the content of this volume to those
truths and practices that most impacted the process of
my own recovery. The pathway described here I have
first walked. I say this to bring hope to the reader. This

---

[1]I believe it would be helpful to define the phrase "inner healing" as used in
this book. It represents an activity of the Holy Spirit founded upon the sacrifice
of Christ on Calvary. The focus of the Spirit's work in this case involves identifying dysfunctional behavior and the root emotional woundings that cause such
types of personal bondage. Using numerous instruments of grace—such as confession, repentance, prayer, Scripture, and gifted counselors—the Holy Spirit is
able to bring healing to the painful memories and deliverance from strongholds
of sin rooted in past events. This "inner healing" is possible because Jesus Christ
was victorious over *all* forms of sin and brokenness, and this victory is available
to all who turn to Him in humility and obedience.

material is not theoretical, but practical. It does not contain an untested thesis, but is based on the Word of God—truth that is eternally living, that can heal the brokenhearted and set the captives free, that is rooted in the One who is Truth, Jesus Christ.

I would like to express my deep appreciation to my publisher, Leonard Allen and the people at Leafwood, for making this resource available. They have consistently displayed excellence in publishing, as well as a deep commitment to developing resources that help broken people find freedom in Christ. Working with them is a joy.

*Each account described in this volume is true. However, in many cases I have changed names and contexts to protect some very special people.*

## Chapter One

# The Healing Begins

*I* hate pain! For a man in his early forties that confession is far from impressive. Yet it is the bare fact and I may as well admit it. I hate pain in all forms and degrees, having held this conviction for as long as I can remember. My basic approach to pain is simple. Whenever possible avoid it, ignore it, minimize it, or in the more intense phases find an anesthetic. Whatever you do, don't become friendly with it. Pain is an enemy to health, an unwelcome invader into our physical, emotional, mental, and spiritual tranquility. To be more emphatic, pain is evil!

In the not-too-distant past I attended a spiritual retreat at a beautiful and well-known conference center in Colorado. Twenty adults gathered for two weeks of spiritual renewal and rest. About four days into the experience we were brought together for a special meeting. One in our "family of seekers" had a confession to make. This dear man told us that he was a heroin addict. On hearing this, I felt great empathy and hope for our brother's deliverance. But he went on to share that during the beginning of the retreat he was not feeling well, went to the doctor and was diagnosed with contagious hepatitis. My focus and feelings shifted with lightning speed!

My first question was, "What does this mean for me?!" The answer was unexpected and quite frankly ticked me off. The resident nurse announced, "If we have been infected, left untreated it could be fatal." *PAIN!* "The county board of health has been notified and will be quarantining us for the next several days." *MORE PAIN!* "We will all be given a series of shots to inoculate us against the disease." *OUCH!*

My next questions were, "How many shots, and how bad would they hurt?" Are you getting the picture yet? I really don't like pain! When my turn came to get the shots, I was asked whether I wanted them in my arm or hip. What question do you think I asked? You got it! "Where would it be less painful?!"

I have the same feelings about emotional pain. Take, for example, the pain that results from personal rejection. I hate it! To protect myself I have developed a variety of defense mechanisms. I can isolate from others, avoiding all risk of rejection, work hard to please so as not to invoke rejection, develop a "who cares" attitude to insulate myself from potential rejection, or if absolutely necessary, emotionally reject someone before they reject me.

Confessing all of this is not at all easy. Especially

since my resistance mechanism toward pain has remained relatively undetected. As I have said, at the heart of all this has been a conviction that pain is evil. My pain, your pain, the pain of the starving, lonely, depressed, despondent, and dying. It is to be avoided, ignored, hidden, or anesthetized, for it is of no good whatsoever.

## My Personal Wilderness

Beginning in May of 1992, I entered a season of emotional breakdown that was deep, dark, frightening, and the most painful experience of my life. For six months I struggled to maintain even a remote sense of sanity, and following thirty days of inpatient clinical treatment, began a recovery period that lasted over a year. This experience has had a profound effect on all aspects of my life. It has also reached deeply into the lives of my family, friends, and local church.

It was during these dark days that God revealed a very important biblical truth to me: God does not share my opinion of pain. Far from being evil, in a fallen world, pain—whether physical, emotional, mental, or spiritual—is *good*! It is a wonderful gift from a loving God meant to keep us from sure destruction.

Pain, in all its shapes and degrees, is a God-given warning system that kicks in automatically when something is wrong. It is like a smoke alarm, set to go off at the first sign of injury, increasing in intensity in direct proportion to the level of potential harm. In God's divine scheme for the post-fallen world, pain is an attention grabber, demanding our immediate focus and action.

But much like me, most people hate pain, seeing it as an enemy to their happiness. They either shut off the alarm or insulate themselves from the "sound" by developing elaborate, and I might add destructive, coping mechanisms. A coping mechanism can be defined as any behavior that one adopts to hide or avoid pain. By doing this a person simply invests in his or her ongoing deterioration. This is true whether the pain being "silenced" is located in the physical or psycho-spiritual part of the human being.

For years I have had an active and intense work ethic. In my service to the Lord, I went by that unhealthy adage, "I'd rather burnout than rust out." By May of 1992 I was teaching full time at Simpson Graduate School, serving as senior pastor of a church of eight hundred, writing a revision to a previously published work, and preparing for an intensive week of lecturing at Alliance Theological Seminary. In addition I had my normal responsibilities as a husband and father of three.

Looking back, I can see that my anxiety level was incredibly high, and I was operating on pure adrenaline. But, as I had done my entire life, I simply ignored the physical signals from my body and verbal warnings from close friends. My rationale for such behavior was simply "working hard for Jesus." The truth is I was an addicted workaholic, with my personal identity too deeply rooted in my profession and performance. I know that now, but back then I did not have a clue.

My "breakdown" began in late May, with successive stages following within weeks. The first stage was marked by unusual levels of anxiety and fear. For example, I found myself almost paralyzed when crossing a bridge. Quite often I would wake up in the middle of the night in a cold sweat from a horrid nightmare. I took the matter to prayer, even fasting several days, believing it to be an attack of the evil one. But rather than subsiding, the battle simply intensified—yet I pushed on.

The next stage was marked by the first of hundreds of panic attacks. Without warning I would grow lightheaded, my heart would race, and there would be an uncontrollable urge to run in fear. The feelings were irrational, but no amount of self-talk worked. It happened at church, in stores, while driving, at home, almost everywhere. At this stage's worst, panic attacks would occur ten to fifteen times a day and eventually led to my being temporarily homebound. I avoided any place and any person that triggered these very frightening adrenaline rushes.

Next, and almost overnight, I fell into deep depression. I still remember the date the darkness settled in—July 5, 1992. This season was marked by persistent crying, isolation in a darkened bedroom and feelings of dread and black despair. At times I felt totally hopeless, emotionally assaulted with uncontrollable thoughts of a God-less eternal night. For weeks I was unable to read and found Scripture condemning or irrelevant. This only heightened my level of anxiety, panic, fear, and depression. The cycle was set to breed on itself.

The final stage of my illness was marked by obsessive-compulsive thoughts; fear of death by heart failure invaded my mind constantly. To say it was horrible would be understating the case. I added to this nightmare by making self-condemning and shaming statements like, "Where's your faith?"

By mid-July I placed myself under the care of one of my dearest friends, a physician named Thomas Hignell. His efforts and investments in my well-being were tireless. For weeks he called daily, checking in with me and helping Cheryl cope with my illness. He also contacted the elders of my church, the dean of the college, and the district church leaders, canceling all my obligations and responsibilities for an indefinite period of time. Tom demanded isolation, rest, and the most extensive physical examinations possible.

Test results were inconclusive. I was in good physical health. My heart, tested by both EKG and treadmill, was found to be normal. All blood tests were well within normal range for a man my age. Tom concluded that I was emotionally burnt out, brought on by high levels of stress sustained over a long period of time. He prescribed, along with rest and isolation, a medication that would help with anxiety. In addition, he called me regularly and read Scripture to me for over two and a half months! To say the least this friend was a gift from God.

## Improvement Begins

Over time I did experience some improvement. The depression lifted to a degree, and the number of panic attacks decreased. By mid-August I was reading again, and going for short walks around our property. Looking to God for total healing, I began long hours in prayer and Scripture study. In addition I read everything I could find on depression, fear, and obsessive-compulsive thinking. I attacked these enemies in every way I knew. I listened to positive music, confessed positive truths, demanded positive attitudes from those around me, did positive things, and prayed positive prayers.

There was, however, one problem! After several months of this activity, I was still fighting depression, battling fears, and consumed with obsessive thoughts of heart failure. I was not as bad as I had been, but my life was marked by day-to-day survival and very little victory!

One afternoon in late October I was lying upon our couch praying. Suddenly, I sensed the voice of God speaking deep within, and the message was astounding:

*Stop fighting depression, fear, and obsessive-compulsive thinking!*

At first I wanted to rebuke the thought, but deep within I knew it was God. My response was quite simple:

*Tell me what You mean by this Lord.*

Lying there my eyes glanced over to our bookcase, focusing upon a volume purchased some years past but never read. It was *Healing for Damaged Emotions* by David Seamands. Immediately I took down the book and began to read. It turned out to be God's direct guidance for my circumstance. Seamands argues that problems such as mine—fear, depression, obsessive-compulsive thinking and the like—are symptoms, not causes. In other words, they serve a person similar to a fever. They are emotional alarms, signaling deeper and far more destructive wounds in the psycho-spiritual self.

These wounds could have occurred as far back as infancy, and may have been self-inflicted or brought on by significant others in my world. The woundings were hurtful, and as a result I unconsciously developed a rather sophisticated set of coping mechanisms to numb the pain. But over the years these unaddressed wounds began to set off louder and louder alarms, eventuating in my breakdown.

Seamands helped me recognize that the pain of depression, panic and obsessive thinking—as horrible as it may be—was not my enemy. Rather these symptoms were alarms sounding off at full volume, notifying me that something was wrong deep within.

You see, I was actually praying an incorrect prayer. I wanted God to take away the symptoms. But loving me as He does, God never answered such an unwise and destructive request. Instead, He caused me to see that deep emotional wounds were demanding my attention. Unaddressed they would only lead to my destruction. Through the pain of this personal wilderness, God was graciously leading me into a far more important season of healing. It would involve more than simply the elimination of depression, panic, and compulsion. The Lord was setting my feet upon the path of inner healing that would bring change at the very core of my being.

I could finally see it—pain is not an enemy, it is an

ally! Pain is not evil; it is, in an evil world, a necessary good. Within five days I was in Colorado Springs at a Rapha treatment center, beginning a twenty-one-day inpatient program designed to peel back layers of defense mechanisms to uncover hidden and even forgotten wounds. Some of these were forty years old, each needing the touch of the Great Physician.[1]

## Pain Is Good

In the economy of God, pain is good. The Psalmist affirmed this when he wrote in Psalm 119, verses 67 and 71:

> *Before I was afflicted I went astray, but now I obey your word. . . . It was good for me to be afflicted so that I might learn your decrees.*

Here, affliction, which certainly involves pain, was ultimately used to correct and direct the psalmist. Similarly, in Isaiah 38:17, from the familiar account of Hezekiah, we read:

> *Surely it was for my benefit that I suffered such anguish. In your love you have kept me from the pit of destruction, you have put all my sins behind your back.*

---

[1] Rapha is a Christ-centered, inpatient counseling program with centers across the United States. Founded by Robert McGee, their psychiatric initiatives are clearly founded on biblical principles. With McGee, the only correct answer is the biblical one. For information, call 1-800-227-2657.

Dr. Paul Brand has spent over forty years working with those who feel no physical pain—the leprous. *In His Image*, co-authored by Brand and Philip Yancey, has much to say about the value of pain. They write,

> The mechanics of pain resemble those of other sensations: like taste or sight or sound, pain is detected by the nerve ending of receptor cells, translated into a chemical and electrical code and conveyed to the brain where a meaning or interpretation is assigned.
>
> Pain . . . functions with such brutal efficiency that its message can preoccupy the brain and drown out all pleasurable signals. It travels along a hotline, insisting on priority. Moreover its impact can spread out from the brain and ultimately involve the entire body.[2]

Dr. Brand has seen the tortuous effects of those who develop leprosy, losing all sensation of pain. The disease overrides the pain mechanism God made in humans, ignoring and shutting down the entire receptor system. As a result people can be injured and yet they do not feel it. This leads to infection, dysfunction, amputation, and even death.

Brand tells the story of Sadan, a patient who fell asleep while reading. His hand, insensitive to pain, fell against a kerosene lamp, burning down to the tendons. All because he could feel no pain. It is no

---

[2] Paul Brand and Philip Yancey, *In His Image* (Grand Rapids, MI: Zondervan, 1984), pp. 229-230.

wonder Dr. Brand is a fanatic about pain! It is a gracious gift to people. If only we could better understand its purpose!

Our society is filled with people who have suffered deep emotional woundings. The list of injuries that have occurred to people during childhood alone is almost endless. Physical, emotional and sexual abuse; rejection, shaming, manipulation, abandonment; control, motivation by fear, the absence of all positive affirmations. This is only the tip of what is hidden deep within so many, many people of all ages, genders, and classes.

But rather than address the wounds head-on, we are taught to hide, stuff, cope, pretend and, if possible, forget them all together.

Elaborate coping mechanisms are developed to mask the hideous truth. Some of these coping mechanisms are socially acceptable, even applauded as admirable: workaholism, perfectionism, people pleasing, rescuing, performance. Others are more unacceptable, yet in reality no more or less destructive: chemical and alcoholic addictions, sexual addictior s of all types, kleptomania, shopping addictions, eating disorders, isolationism. These represent but some of the many ways unaddressed and ignored woundings translate into dysfunctional behavior.

Over time and under stressful situations other symptoms appear: rage, fear, panic, phobias, depression, psychosis, neurosis and aggression, to name a few.

I look at the dear people in my congregation and I see the symptoms of emotional injury everywhere. I see wounded people who have tried for years to bury memories and escape their painful pasts, but it just has not worked. As a result these beautiful blood-bought brothers and sisters live in bondage, while pretending that everything is fine. God has now given me eyes to see the truth and praise His name; the truth does set people free!

There is good news! Great news! Christ wants to bring healing to the wounds that keep us emotionally crippled. He wants to go far beyond symptoms and coping mechanisms. He desires to touch us at the very heart of our woundings. Unbound by time, Jesus, through the cross, is able and willing to heal our damaged emotions. He can take us back to the painful past and anoint our emotional wounds with the oil of His healing.

Jesus did so much more than forgive us of sins at Calvary. Isaiah prophesied that there He would also carry ᴜᴜᴜ infirmities and sorrows (53:4). He would be scourged, and from those wounds would come our healing. This healing is not limited to our sinful souls and sick physical bodies. Jesus is God's answer for the emotionally abused and broken. His riches are un-searchable and include the healing so many of us desperately need.

Are you in pain? Don't try to hide it; don't stifle your emotions or develop some elaborate coping mechanism—it won't work! The answer is quite simple, though far from easy. Permit Christ Jesus to shine His light into the inner recesses of your hidden self. With that surrender, the healing begins!

## Chapter Two

# The Path Toward Wholeness

*J*essica Lorenzo has been a close friend since God caused our paths to cross in the early 1980s. My family and I were living in Pennsylvania where I was pastor of a United Methodist congregation. Jessica and her husband Paul were part of a hard-rock subculture, caught in the bondage and brokenness of drugs. Each was a member of an area band hoping to make it big, but living the godless night life of area bars and honkey-tonks.

Jessica's mother began attending our church and was wonderfully converted to Christ. Her testimony ultimately moved Jessica to visit our Sunday morning service. I'll never forget seeing her seated beside her mother, wearing tattered jeans, a T-shirt and a man's overcoat, with her hair dyed purple. Paul was not with her, uninterested in this "Jesus thing." But be assured of this, the Lord was very interested in them!

Over time my wife and I had the blessing of leading both Jessica and Paul to Christ. We personally invested in their discipleship training, which opened the door for what is a special relationship today.

The change in the Lorenzo's lives was obvious and radical. Separating from their past lifestyle, God set them free from drugs, alcohol and other destructive trappings of the rock culture. Paul and Jessica began using their talents for the Lord and brought several friends to a saving relationship with the Lord Jesus Christ.

Jessica had always been a very outgoing, helpful person. She was quick to serve, upbeat with everyone and hungry to give her all to the Lord. All of this added to our absolute shock when we were told she suffered a breakdown and was in a psychiatric hospital.

What happened, and why did no one see it coming? At first Jessica experienced increasing amounts of fear and sudden outbursts of rage. In the beginning she was able to control these emotions, but before long they controlled her. Initial sessions with a therapist led to the decision for inpatient care. Suicidal thoughts began to dominate much of Jessica's thinking.

It was not long before deep emotional woundings were uncovered, sending Jessica into a long period of Christ-centered treatment and recovery. Hidden from everyone was a dark and abusive past. Like countless people in our society, Jessica's childhood was marked by physical, emotional, and sexual abuse.

When Jessica accepted Christ, she experienced genuine forgiveness for her past sin. But the wounds and shame of her childhood experiences were a haunting and painful memory. To cope, Jessica sought to gain approval and worth through her performance. She was also a chronic people pleaser. She was constantly helping others and deathly afraid of rejection. For years it seemed that Jessica could handle her past by stifling the emotional pain of past woundings with more and more activity.

However, as so often happens to victims of parental dysfunction, the hiding and coping ultimately led to breakdown. Praise the Lord that in God's grace Jessica was led step by step to new freedom. But it took hard work, lots of prayer, and many months of vulnerability before the Lord, to bring the necessary inner healing.

I pastor a congregation of over eight hundred men, women, and children. It would not be an exaggeration to state that over seventy-five percent carry wounds of victimization. It is, of course, well hidden, covered over with the appropriate "religious" cosmetics. But just below the surface of many lives is an emotional storm. This storm blows harder in some than others, more frequently at times than others. But the tempest is there![1]

The dysfunction caused by emotional woundings is epidemic. It is also demonic, an all-out attack of Satan to:

a) destroy people made in God's image;

---

[1] After preaching a twelve-week series on inner healing, we initiated a fifteen-week program for support and healing to any adult struggling with emotional wounds. The level of participation was staggering, opening our eyes to the extent of emotional distress in people's lives and their willingness to seek help when it is provided.

b) keep people trapped in shame; and
c) pass dysfunction on to their children and
their children's children.

If you or someone you love is a victim of emotional,
physical and/or spiritual abuse, there is help in Jesus
Christ. He came to set the captives free! Salvation
through Him is far more than forgiveness of sins and
a ticket to heaven. Salvation includes healing: physical, spiritual, and emotional. In Isaiah 53 we are told
that the suffering servant would bear not only our
iniquities, but our griefs and sorrows too!

## Steps to Inner Healing

### STEP ONE: Admit That Something Is Wrong!

Like all journeys, the path to inner healing begins
with the first step: *admit that something is wrong!* To get
at the root, you must first recognize that you see the
fruit. In this case it is the fruit of dysfunction. Does an
honest appraisal of your life reveal any of the following?

Symptoms:
  rage
  uncontrollable fear
  depression
  phobias
  distrust
  defensiveness
  inability to receive criticism
  blaming

inability to be intimate
relational isolation
high levels of anxiety
panic attacks
thoughts of suicide
thoughts of violence
desire to run away
abusive behavior

Coping Mechanisms (behaviors embraced to hide or mask the pain of the past):
performance
workaholism
people pleasing
addiction to approval
addiction to attention
rescuing
chronic problem to gain attention
chronic problem solving
manipulation
lust for control
perfectionism
chemical abuse
alcohol abuse
sexual addiction
eating disorder
shopping addiction
kleptomania
child abuse
gambling addiction

Certainly any one or more of these problems are in

themselves destructive. But they actually represent symptoms of much deeper woundings. Addressing only the symptoms may eliminate certain behaviors, but the root wounding will eventually bring forth fruit in a different area. Remember the appearance of "fruit" must lead you to find and eliminate the root. In cases such as these the root is often emotional woundings, and the process of elimination is what I refer to as inner healing.

One principle must be followed to experience wholeness: whatever is in the darkness must be brought into the light of Christ. To hide, deny, run, or cope only enhances the enemy's plan of destruction.

Admitting that you are seeing the fruit of dysfunction brings it out into the light where Jesus can heal. For me it began by admitting two things:

1. I was struggling with depression and fear.
2. I was a workaholic, seeking personal worth through performance.[2]

---

[2] I cannot over-emphasize the importance of getting professional help in this process. While in some cases an individual can walk the path of healing with Christ alone, most need intervention from professionals. Depending on the level of dysfunction and pain it could mean any of the following: a pastoral counselor, therapist, psychologist, psychiatrist, short- or long-term inpatient programs, support groups for eating disorders, chemical dependency, twelve-step programs, or the like. For me the process involved an inpatient program, intensive spiritual retreat and weekly therapy. Regardless of the route you choose, be *sure* it is totally Christ-centered, biblically based and balanced, addressing all aspects of our humanity—physical, spiritual, emotional, and mental. Ask hard questions before beginning treatment with someone. Know up front their position on Christ-centered care and the supernatural. Remember—they work for you, so be assertive about where they stand and what they attempt to do in therapy.

You may find that those closest to you can help with your "fruit inspection." My wife and friends could see things I could not. Once I opened up to their opinion, I was able to see some very destructive behavior on my part. Though still unsure as to what lay behind the behavior, I began to recognize that somewhere deep within were problems that needed serious attention.

### STEP TWO: Realize That Apart from Jesus Christ, You Can Do Nothing

In your own strength you are powerless to bring about inner healing. Certainly bookstores are filled with self-help books aimed at behavior modification. But, when the root cause of dysfunctional behavior is an emotional wounding, the best help such approaches offer is "picking fruit." They cannot and do not get to the root issues of which the fruit is symptomatic. To receive genuine and complete healing, you must confess that *on your own you are powerless to change.*

How many times I have watched the futility of self-effort in breaking bondage or bringing inner healing. Take Joe Rogers for example. For years his wife Linda agonized as alcohol ravaged not only her husband, but indirectly her entire family. She tried to address the issue with Joe, but he constantly denied any drinking problem. His response was always the same: "There's nothing wrong with a drink now and then. Even the Apostle Paul says, 'a little wine is good for the stomach.' "

But Joe was drinking more than a little and the destructive power of alcohol was taking its toll.

For years Joe's drinking worsened until it threatened his health, marriage, and employment. Finally, when he hit what was seemingly the bottom, Joe admitted, "I have a problem." I remember well, because Linda called me to the house for pastoral care and advice. There Joe sat, weeping on the couch with Linda at his side.

This was obviously a big step toward healing. Joe was admitting that he had a serious problem. It was undeniably a great breakthrough. But as I counseled Joe it became increasingly clear that he was not willing to move to step two, admitting he was powerless to change on his own. Joe was proud and determined, saying, "I got myself into this mess, I can get myself out." He refused any and all forms of help and intervention. Joe was going to beat this by flying solo. The result? He crashed before ever getting off the runway!

There are three obvious reasons why a person cannot go it alone in healing damaged emotions.

First, as stated before, dysfunction is symptomatic. For Joe, alcoholism was a symptom of deep darkness brought on by emotional wounding. Attack the behavior all you will, the darkness remains to rule and destroy.

Secondly, dysfunctional behavior is rooted in sin. Even if the original wounding was inflicted by another, the way most people choose to cope is sinful. And as Paul says, apart from the power of Christ, sin controls you, you don't control it!

*Don't you know that when you offer yourselves to someone to obey him as slaves, you are slaves to that*

> one whom you obey—whether you are slaves to sin,
> which leads to death? (Romans 6:16)

Scripture repeatedly affirms this principle, and the metaphor of slavery is perfect. Sin controls, uses, and ultimately destroys. Even in the believer's life, hidden woundings become ground that the enemy often occupies. From such strongholds he viciously attacks, and in one's own strength a person is powerless to experience freedom.

Third, Jesus taught that changing behavior is not the key to wholeness. Behavior is merely the outside of the cup (Matthew 23:25-26). The seedbed of dysfunction, in the words of the Lord, comes from "within, out of men's hearts" (Mark 7:21). And apart from surgery at this level, long-term freedom is impossible. Again, in one's own strength even the best efforts are ultimately futile. Inner healing never truly comes by mere human strength. Once you admit this horrible bad news, you have made a giant step forward. And what comes next is the greatest news of all.

### STEP THREE: Believe That Nothing Is Impossible with God

While on your own you are powerless to change, with God all things are possible (Luke 1:37)! No matter how dark the circumstance or disabling the dysfunction, God has made a way to wholeness. Jesus Christ, God's beloved Son, defeated Satan at the cross and has since put all things under His feet (Colossians 2:13-15; Ephesians 1:22). As a result people can, by accepting Christ, receive a salvation that is beyond description. In Jesus, God has provided all one needs to live free from emotional bondage, victorious in this life (Ephesians 1:3; 2 Peter 1:3).

This salvation includes the ongoing transformation of the inner being (2 Corinthians 3:17-18). By recognizing this you are able to surrender to Christ all your woundings, whether inflicted by others or by yourself. The Lord's response to such vulnerability, honesty, and surrender is faithful. He will in His way and time and strength work to bring deliverance and complete freedom. While nothing you can do on earth could help, Jesus has the authority of heaven to heal your dark memories and damaged emotions.

Take the Apostle Paul as an example. The record of his life in Acts gives clear evidence that he was a dysfunctional man before meeting Christ. He was a racial bigot who found his identity in performance, a man filled with anger and guilty of murder. But then he met Jesus and was converted on the road to Damascus (Acts 9). Over time the Lord brought about a total transformation in Paul's life. He rooted his identity in Christ and bore the fruit of servanthood, peace, love for all men and women, and—ultimately—martyrdom. Paul surrendered to Christ and allowed Him to touch the deepest and darkest parts of his inner being. The lies and wounds that lurked within him were rooted out, and in their place came new life, causing Paul to say, "I can do everything through him who gives me strength" (Philippians 4:13). My friend, to move on toward inner wholeness, exercise the faith to believe that what Jesus has done for others, He will do for you!

### STEP FOUR: Let the Holy Spirit Be Your Guide

Ask the Holy Spirit to walk you through the process of healing by revealing the source of your pain. By this time you should be far beyond symptoms. You are opening up to truth revealed in the innermost parts of your life. Like David of old you cry out, "Search me, O God, and know my heart" (Psalm 139:23). This is unquestionably risky and potentially very painful. You are allowing the Holy Spirit to shine light upon the dark, painful, hidden events of your life. The purpose: to reveal those events that are at the very core of your feelings of shame, unworthiness, and anger.

If you let Him, the Holy Spirit will unveil the secret and shameful ways of your past. Why? That you might renounce Satan's claim to that part of your life and move on to wholeness in Christ Jesus. Instead of denial that leads to dysfunction, what results is healing that brings freedom and newness of life.

In John 14 we read our Lord's promise to send the Holy Spirit. The Spirit would indwell believers for many purposes, including serving as a counselor, willing to reveal the truth (14:15-16). In John 16:13 Jesus assured His followers that the Holy Spirit would guide the believer into all truth. In theology, this ongoing journey is called sanctification, which in its Greek root means "to be separate" or "to be set apart for a purpose." Traditionally it signifies the activity of the Holy Spirit whereby He empowers believers to cooperate in becoming like Jesus in attitude, action, and appetite. This process involves a crisis of repentance and the tearing down of old, sinful patterns of behavior and belief and the continual renewing of the mind which enables a person to seek after holiness in keeping with the new nature one receives upon accepting the Lord. As it relates to emotional/relational dysfunction, it is helpful to refer to this journey as the process of inner healing. He, the Spirit, reveals the truth about the lies that bind us, then sets us free to live the life that transforms.

From all outward appearances Julie was a mature Christian wife, mother, and minister. She was raised in a Christian home, trained at a Christian college, was married to a young pastor and was serving in a successful church. That was what everyone knew of her, and often Julie was the reference point for godliness in a young woman. And with genuine humility this was Julie's assessment of her own life, with all glory going to Christ.

But in the fall of 1993, Julie began to experience a growing sense of rage. It manifested itself particularly in outbursts of anger toward her small children. Her verbal scoldings grew abusive and shame-based, and the guilt she felt over her behavior was unbearable. The nagging question was, Why? In desperation she sought out an area pastor and his wife for help.

Her assignment after the first session was interesting and opened the door for deep inner healing. She was asked to do two things:

1. To pray, asking the Holy Spirit to bring to her memory any events from her past that brought feelings of shame, unworthiness, and failure.

2. To write these down in an autobiographical format in order to remember what the Spirit revealed.

This is a technique similar to one used in my own therapy, so I know the power it can bring to inner healing.

From there, week by week, session by session, Julie would detail what the Spirit revealed, one incident at a time. Her counselors were sensitive, allowing Julie to express the emotion of the event, pray for the Spirit's healing and replace all lies with the truth of God's word.[3]

Julie publicly gave testimony to the deep work God was doing, healing the wounds of her past. She was

---

[3] Once again I must emphasize the importance of receiving help from trained, spiritually mature counselors. Beside the obvious reasons, I want to mention two significant problems faced in the inner healing process. First, Satan is not passive as an individual pursues wholeness. He can and does flood a person's mind with thoughts that are not based in truth. A counselor must be able to discern and disarm all deceitful demonic interference. Recognizing that this battle "is not against flesh and blood," spiritual maturity and biblical armor are essential. Only the counselor who is sensitive to the Holy Spirit's role in bringing about freedom will be effective.

Secondly, countless individuals have been misguided by counselors who lead the broken into "contrived memories." Such therapists move too quickly to "diagnose" root woundings, because the client profile fits certain aspects of specific victimization. For example, a dear friend was asked by her therapist to share childhood memories. She commented to the counselor that she had few memories of her early years. To this the "professional" immediately concluded that this woman had been sexually abused. The therapist then spoke into her mind memories which simply had not happened. It was not a case of client denial, but rather unethical and unhealthy therapeutic practice. Such fraudulent behavior is far from uncommon and not restricted to non-Christian professionals. Therefore, seek out counselors prayerfully and require extensive recommendations from people who are trusted in the field.

set free from suppressed rage linked to a domineering, controlling father who was both religiously legalistic and abusive. For him performance was all that mattered, trapping Julie in a lifestyle of perfection and approval long into her adulthood. But the grace of Jesus applied by the Holy Spirit set her free within, changing Julie's behavior.

It is critical to mention here that it is the Holy Spirit who must reveal the source of pain. Rest in that trust. Don't worry over your past. Don't try to turn over every potential rock or look in every dark corner. He will faithfully guide the process. Do not allow an obsessive personality to kick in to the point that you suffer from the "paralysis of analysis." The Spirit is faithful to reveal deep, hidden woundings. Don't rush ahead and frustrate the process. You may think there are no past experiences or memories that haunt you. That may well be, but let the Holy Spirit show you the truth. You may be surprised at the foothold Satan has in your inner being from events of the past.

### STEP FIVE: *Express Your Emotions before the Lord*

As the Holy Spirit reveals the wounds of the past, take time to express your emotions honestly before the Lord. People, particularly Christians, are often dishonest about their emotions. Parents, and even some pastors, have  encouraged hurt, violated, or abused individuals to stifle their feelings. Feelings are seen as unreliable; if they include anger, rage, fear, or sorrow, they are even considered sinful! Emotions are suppressed, stuffed into some hidden place deep within. A blanket of forgiveness is quickly thrown over every wounding that ever occurred, in an effort to be truly Christlike.

But the potential for long-term emotional dysfunction is tremendous. Behind a facade of peace, often propped up by performance, is a growing emotional storm. When it ultimately breaks through the veil of pretense, it comes with hurricane force.

What is the Christlike way to handle any and all levels of victimization? Immediately our minds go to passages on forgiveness (Matthew 6:14; Matthew 18:15-35; Luke 6:37). Jesus taught that forgiveness is clearly a requirement of the kingdom. But, I would argue that true forgiveness involves more than removing the moral hindrance between the offender and the offended. It often requires time before God where the emotions of the offense are expressed and then placed at the foot of the cross. That, I believe, is the Christlike pattern.

In Luke 22:39-46, the account of our Lord's agony in Gethsemane, we see that *before* Jesus uttered words of forgiveness from the cross, He anguished in Gethsemane before the Father. That anguish was the outpouring of emotional stress, anticipating betrayal, rejection, mockery, abuse, ending in a savage death. Jesus did not vent this toward His offenders, but poured out His feelings before the Father. The portrait in Scripture is one of deep, emotional agony. In contemporary terms, He was saying, "Father, this hurts! I feel like I am going to die inside. Is there any other way?"

Only after unloading the agonizing emotional and spiritual turmoil did Jesus offer forgiveness to those who crucified Him. Instead of stifling His feelings, simply expressing the correct theological requirement of forgiveness, Jesus let His emotions spill out before God. As a result, when from the cross He said, "Father, forgive them, for they do not know what they are doing" (Luke 23:34), there was no hidden bitterness or resentment. He had already surrendered His hurt to God during those hours of emotional anguish.

I believe the Lord modeled a crucial and often neglected step on the path toward inner healing. If you or anyone else has been emotionally violated, take time to go to the cross and anguish in prayer before the Lord. He understands. Express your anger and fear, grieve your losses—it's okay! It's the right thing to do. Let it all out before the Lord. Believe me, He can and wants to take it!

At one point in my recovery I experienced a season of deep weeping before the Lord over certain aspects of my childhood. I particularly grieved not having had an intimate relationship with my father. During this season of anguish I grieved over missing out on playing catch, fishing trips, outings to the ball park, and all other opportunities a father and son have to build intimacy. Then and only then could I genuinely forgive my dad. Oh, I mentally had done that years before. But deep inside was a wound never expressed. It led to serious dysfunction and was the seed of my personal wilderness. But after that season of safe anguishing before the Lord, the moral hindrance was gone—genuinely set aside and freedom swept in. I could now truly forgive my father and love him more than ever before.

There are two important things about this step:

First, express your emotions before God, not the offender. Having a therapist or counselor present can be helpful, but the key is to unload before Him. He understands and can handle your anger, rage, fear, doubt, and whatever else. If you need to confront the people who offended you, let the Lord orchestrate the meeting. In His time and place, you will be able to deal honestly with that person, yet remain Christlike and full of grace. For me, God led my dad to Colorado, where a spirit of repentance fell upon him, and forgiveness flowed from the depths of my soul! That was God at work!

Secondly, bathe this season in prayer. Jesus did and for good reason. When the anguish begins to surface you may feel like the disciples did in Gethsemane. Ready to betray, strike out, run, or deny. Pray that you will not enter into that temptation! Stay before the Lord, and let the emotional release take place.

### STEP SIX: *Extend Forgiveness*

One biblical principle of inner healing is unquestionable. Forgiveness must be extended to all who have victimized you, and forgiveness must be sought from all you have offended. This step is so critical that I have dedicated the next chapter to this subject, but for now, I want to discuss a few basic issues relating to forgiveness.

More than once I have counseled a person on the critical nature of forgiveness, only to have them respond, "Never! Not after what that person did to me!" Very often the crime against the individual was in fact hideous: child molestation, abandonment, sexual abuse, adultery. Such sins are deep violations that leave painful wounds. They are also root causes of dysfunction that bring people to counseling in the first place.

To suggest forgiving someone for such sins even after dealing with the emotional pain seems impossible. One common hesitation stems from the misconception that forgiveness somehow erases the offender's responsibility. That is not true. Forgiveness is removing the moral hindrance that stands between you and your abuser, leaving the consequences in the hands of God. Wounded people often see their bitterness or hatred as a power that keeps them from being hurt again, a sort of protection. For Christians, God is our protector and the love of Christ our model.

Another problem is that people do not recognize that unforgiveness is actually damaging to them, the offended. Jesus said that failing to forgive places one in the hands of the tormentors (Matthew 18:21-35). Failing to forgive, no matter how horrible the offense, does lead to personal torment. It is the seedbed of anger, bitterness, fear, revenge, jealousy, and depression. Instead of your victimizer being the prisoner of your unforgiveness, you are! This is why it is so important that you pour out the emotional pain before the Lord, and then in the power of Christ, freely extend forgiveness. Forgiving sets you free!

There are four final thoughts to be considered regarding forgiveness:

1. It does involve a certain degree of risk, includ-

ing the possibility of being hurt again. For example, if you forgive an unfaithful spouse, there is the chance that he or she could be unfaithful again. If the abuse you have suffered recurs, you may need to remove yourself from the situation—while still extending forgiveness for the past offense.

2. Forgiving is not forgetting. Our brains retain a record of all past events. When touched by the Spirit, the pain of the event will be gone, though the memory will remain.

3. Forgiving is not excusing, either. It is not rationalizing away your abuser's responsibility because of the extenuating circumstances that led to your victimization. It is true, many perpetrators were themselves victims; our hearts should go out with hope for their healing. A sexual addiction, for example, may not be a person's fault. Absence of intimacy in childhood or sexual abuse may have led them to this dysfunction. But their abusive actions are still their responsibility. Forgiveness means removing the hindrance, not rationalizing the offense and offender's responsibility away.

4. Finally, forgiveness is not pretending that the event never happened. Some therapists use a very unbiblical form of visualization in inner healing: they encourage people to return to the

event in their mind, picturing Jesus undoing what happened. They call this "changing the pictures" on the walls of their memory. This is both unbiblical and unhealthy. Jesus can heal the emotional scars caused by rape. But He doesn't rewrite history so that a person can give a testimony of being un-raped! Your history stands as it is. But Jesus can heal the wounds of victimization, giving you the power to genuinely say, "I am free, and in the name of Jesus I set you free. You are forgiven."

## Summary

In John 3:8 there is record of Jesus teaching a critical principle of the Holy Spirit's ministry: "The wind blows wherever it pleases. You hear its sound, but cannot tell where it comes from or where it is going. So it is with everyone born of the Spirit."

While the context is Jesus discussing the born-again experience with Nicodemus, there is a more general principle within the text. The ministry of the Holy Spirit in the life of an individual is sovereign. That sovereign activity has a paradoxical nature to it, predictable and unpredictable at the same time.

The Holy Spirit ministers predictably. All He says and does will be consistent with the witness of Scripture. He always affirms truth and constantly bears witness to the unsearchable riches of Christ Jesus—of this you can be sure. In fact, the easiest way to test a spiritual work is by looking for those two qualities: an emphasis on truth and the centrality of Christ.

But at the same time the Holy Spirit's work is unpredictable. While I have presented steps along the path to inner healing in this chapter, they are not cut and dried. You must not see each step as an ingredient within a recipe, guaranteed to work precisely in the same way with every person. No, the Holy Spirit works as He wills, once we open ourselves to the process. He determines what issues to address, the pace and timing of healing, the various instruments to use in the process and the degree of freedom that results, given our ongoing cooperation. He often overlaps the steps in the process, finishing one issue as you are in the middle of another while starting to face a third.

For some people crisis moments are key instruments of healing grace. For others the Holy Spirit uses a book, a counselor, intensive prayer therapy, or a spiritual retreat. Again, He is in control, appropriately applying the work of Christ in the specific way best suited to the individual.

But I speak for hundreds who have received inner healing or are beginning the process by quoting Second Corinthians 3:17-18:

> *Now the Lord is the Spirit, and where the Spirit of the Lord is, there is freedom. And we, who with unveiled faces all reflect the Lord's glory, are being transformed into his likeness with ever-increasing glory, which comes from the Lord, who is the Spirit.*

That's freedom!

*Chapter Three*

# Focusing on Forgiveness

orgiveness is directly related to our emotional well-being. Jesus clearly taught that its importance cannot be over-emphasized or its practice over-done. Jesus instructed Peter that forgiveness must be extended regardless of the number of times one had been offended (Matthew 18:21-22). This is God's way with repentant people, and it must be our way as well. And, as mentioned in the previous chapter, failure to forgive ultimately leads to torment (18:34).

Freda Ellison was a woman bound by the torment of unforgiveness. I met her while serving as a pastor in a small western Pennsylvania village. It was a friendly community, located in the rural farmlands. The village bragged of one store, a post office, a gas station, two churches, and some wonderful people.

There were many fine qualities about life in a

country village. But there was one major problem familiar to many small towns: almost everyone made it their business to know everyone else's business. Gossip was epidemic! And, I might add, it did not stop at the doors of the church. It entered right in, as comfortable there as at the store, post office, and gas station.

As the new pastor, I visited from house to house, getting to know area people and inviting them to church. Freda Ellison lived in a trailer about three miles from the village. I remember my first visit well. Freda came to the door and welcomed me into her modest home. Our time together was initially pleasant, talking mostly about each other's background and personal history.

But the atmosphere took an unmistakable turn when I invited Freda to our church. "Never!" was her immediate and intense reply. I was so stunned by her reaction that I made my excuses and left as quickly as possible. The nerve I touched was obviously raw, but my lack of experience motivated me to politely back away before things got worse.

Over the next year I visited Freda several times, hoping to build a foundation for her conversion. Only after numerous conversations did she share the reason for her attitude about the local church. Years before one of her daughters became pregnant out of wedlock. At the time her family attended the church and was somewhat active in the youth program. But when they most needed the comfort and ministry of the body of Christ, her family received harshness and judgment instead. Freda's daughter became the object of malicious gossip from several leaders within the congregation. As a result, Freda and her family left the congregation, deeply wounded and shamed.

Several points need to be emphasized about this incident. First, sexual intercourse outside of marriage is sin. That is made unmistakably clear in Scripture. But forgiveness is clearly God's prescription for the broken, not scorn and slanderous shaming. Secondly, forgiveness was also the biblical requirement for Freda relative to those people who were so brutal toward her daughter. As difficult as it may be, it is the way of our Lord and must be the way of His followers.

But as far as Freda was concerned, extending forgiveness was impossible! "What they did was far beyond forgetting or setting aside!" And so for years she held the memory of their sin deep in her heart. They were going to stay in the bondage of her unforgiveness forever. But the truth was, Freda was the one in chains. Bitter, vengeful, and full of hate, she was in emotional torment because she refused to forgive. I believe it also affected her health, particularly problems with arthritis and chronic back pain. And it was unquestionably a barrier between Freda and her relationship with God.

I left that congregation after four years, and Freda was unmoved in her resolve. Forgiveness was out of the question. Unfortunately, so was her own well-being—emotionally, spiritually, relationally, and physically.

No matter how great the offense or abuse, along the path to inner healing lies the decision to forgive. In this chapter I want you to consider four aspects of forgiveness that are essential to our emotional well-being.

## 1. Do Not Move to Forgiveness Too Quickly

As my sister and I were growing up it was made crystal clear that jumping on beds was unacceptable. Mom left no question in our minds as to the consequence of breaking the household rules: "the spankings would begin." One day while Mom was in the basement washing, Bonny and I chose to chance it! We began to bounce with glee on our parents' bed. Higher and higher! Faster and faster! Two children were joyfully reckless in abandonment. Suddenly, Bonny, bouncing too close to the edge, came down with full force, hitting her tailbone on the corner of the footboard.

The pain must have been excruciating, for she cried out immediately, long and loud. I jumped to her side and began to beg, "Please don't cry, please! Laugh! Look at this funny face! Laugh! Ha, ha, ha!"

My goal was simple self-preservation. If she did not stop crying, Mom would hear and that meant only one thing—soon we would both be crying. I did everything I could to silence her cries, in an effort to keep my own sin in hiding. It did not work!

I have been in vocational Christian ministry for eighteen years now. My responsibilities have been those of pastor, evangelist, educator, and administrator. In all these years, from each of the different perspectives of ministry, one truth stands out. God's people are very uncomfortable with vulnerability. When someone begins to express deep feelings of emotional wounding, people send the same message I did to my sister: "Please don't hurt, not here, not now." Why? Because in some way it may bring to the surface their own hidden pain.

The people of Christ are made up of former liars, adulterers, fornicators, cheats, slanderers, bigots, and addicts of all sorts. Before Christ, all had the characteristics of the ungodly: anger, hatred, jealousy, envy, rage, and malice. Every single member of the body of Christ was dead in sin at one point. But through repentance and faith in Jesus Christ, their lives were transformed.

Once converted, every new believer is taught about holiness and godly living. Some learn these truths from an unbiblical base of legalism. Others are schooled in the glory of God's grace and unmerited favor that positionally gives a Christian righteousness which practically transforms them day by day through the ongoing work of the Holy Spirit. Either way, the message of the church is clear. Sin in all forms is unacceptable and destructive.

In far too many congregations, people respond to the call to holiness in a sinful and unhealthy manner—they hide! They put on the cosmetic of "religiosity" in church. Though their private lives are often inconsistent with the Christian faith, their public lives appear wonderfully in line with biblical maturity. They know the proper words, serve in the proper ways, sing the appropriate songs, and faithfully attend the scheduled services. All the while they are struggling with sin and past wounds, which eventually eat away at the core of their lives. Emotionally, these people are "held together with chewing gum and bailing wire." Any disruption is capable of putting their entire pretense at risk.

The blame for this lies at the feet of church leadership. Shaming messages are all too often communicated with this type of rebuke: "Don't be caught in sin, it will cost your reputation, position in the local church, and admiration of fellow believers." Such pressure simply keeps people from openness and vulnerability. Behind a facade of "perfection" is a virtual thorn thicket of sin and pain. Believers are often afraid to open up for fear of rejection.

Darren came to our congregation with deep emotional woundings from an abusive childhood. For years he carried the memories of beatings, being openly shamed, even being tied in a closet for hours as a form of punishment. Darren did not trust men, was confused about his identity, and lived in constant fear.

We led Darren into one of our growth groups, thinking it would be a place of acceptance and healing. Though scared to death he took the risk. Our growth groups regularly begin by asking the Wesleyan question, "How are things with your soul?" When it came time for Darren, he opened up, sharing just the surface of his broken past. Immediately people became extremely uncomfortable with the "high" level of emotion. So, instead of listening, weeping with him over his deep pain, they tried to "stuff" what was happening. How did they do that? By insisting that Darren must forgive.

You may say, "Well isn't that the answer?" In due

time, yes. But Darren was in deep pain and needed to be honest about his hurt and anger at his father. It was ruining his life! Instead of allowing him a "Gethsemane" experience, the people in the group insisted that he move immediately to forgiveness. But, as mentioned previously, true forgiveness in some cases comes only after an individual has released his or her pain before the Lord. Believers should be patient, allowing the Holy Spirit to do that deeply needed work.

In *Worry Free Living*, Frank Minirth, Paul Meier, and Don Hawkins tell the story of Linda, a woman in deep depression.[1] Like most people suffering from this problem, Linda was hiding rage at someone. But she insisted that she was the problem, and certainly her husband was nothing but a support. Weeks of therapy revealed that her husband was in fact a manipulator, insensitive, and a user. At first she vehemently denied this, continuing to stifle her emotions.

But ultimately the floodgates opened and Linda exploded in anger and rage as she finally admitted the truth. This emotional display continued for days, but it was a type of "Gethsemane" experience for her. Once emptied of this suppressed rage, Linda was willing and able to take the only biblical course of action: extend forgiveness.

Most Christians are far too insecure to allow such vulnerability and honesty in their midst. Encouraging such an atmosphere of emotional openness may cause other Christians to unexpectedly break through

---

[1] Frank Minirth, Paul Meier and Don Hawkins, *Worry Free Living* (Nashville, TN: Thomas Nelson, 1989), pp. 19-22.

to their own pain. That fear motivates people to "stuff" their emotions, discouraging vulnerability in others. "Let's all just forgive and forget!"

The Church is not a haven for sinless saints. Though redeemed by Christ, there is still a lot of deep work to be done in countless lives. But it requires openness and a safe atmosphere where people can get in touch with their pain. When that happens, true forgiveness will flow out like the river Christ intended. But encouraging a person to forgive before they have had the opportunity to unleash emotional pain at the cross of Christ is premature and unhealthy.

## 2. *Start by Forgiving God*

Let me begin by stating the theologically obvious: God cannot and does not sin. His very nature is marked by perfect holiness in every attribute and action that emanates from His being. God is perfect in love, mercy, and grace. He is righteous, just, and faithful. It is theologically impossible for anyone ever to point to God and justifiably call Him on any transgression. God is infinite in knowledge, wisdom, and power, eternally good in all He is and does. God cannot and does not sin! Let me repeat that again: God cannot and does not sin!

However, there are countless men, women, and children in this world who are angry at God. They feel let down by Him, abandoned or left unprotected at a time when they needed Him most. Some people suppress their feelings, while others are quite vocal, openly turning their backs on God in response to what they believe was a failure on His part.

Let's face it, there is an undeniable tension in the Christian life. Countless Scriptures assure believers of God's love, concern, and protection. Christians are promised angelic care, divine intervention, shelter in times of storm, and a yoke that is easy and light. Christian biographies are filled with wonderful tales of divine intervention in the hour of trial. The promises of God are true and should be confidently embraced by all believers.

But many Christians face experiences that seem to be in direct contradiction to these truths. Through no fault of their own, Christian women are raped, Christian husbands die prematurely, Christian children suffer from terminal cancer, Christian senior citizens agonize with Alzheimer's disease, and Christian families encounter all forms of violence.

Well-meaning pastors try to help by quickly invoking Scriptures that assure God's sovereignty and the promise of "ultimate" good resulting from any and all tragedy. While some Christian victims are strong enough to hold to these truths, most obligingly nod their heads while suppressing a deep-seated emotional rage. "Where were You, God? How could You let this happen to me?"

Most Christian victims realize that their feelings are inappropriate and so they stifle them, hoping that over time the pain will just go away. This approach is more often than not encouraged by fellow believers. "Have faith, trust, believe, and everything will turn out just fine. Praise the Lord!"

I believe stifling emotions and failing to address the pain of victimization is unhealthy and unbiblical. It is unhealthy in that suppressed anger sooner or later shows its ugly head in some other form. It may be depression or misdirected rage or fear. It may be coping mechanisms like performance, busyness, or one of any number of addictions. Anger unaddressed and suppressed always leads to trouble! Pious platitudes, as theologically correct as they may be, are not always the first steps to overcoming emotional wounding.

I also believe that suppressing anger, even when it is directed at God, is unbiblical. Take Job for example. For three-quarters of that book he points his finger at God. He certainly did not do it in a disrespectful or cursing way. But Job let God know that he felt his lot was totally unjustified and unfair. In chapter 9, Job admits that no mortal can question God's actions, because He is so great and mighty. But he then says, "If only there were someone . . . to remove God's rod from me, so that his terror would frighten me no more; Then I would speak up" (Job 9:33-35).

Then Job says, "I will give free rein to my complaint" (10:1). He goes on to present his case. While recognizing God's wisdom, justice, and righteousness, Job still cries out to God, "I've been wronged."

It is easy to find similar laments throughout the Psalms. In the first nine verses of Psalm 77, the writer cries out with deep agony, "Will the Lord reject forever? Will he never show his favor again? Has his unfailing love vanished forever? Has his promise failed for all time? Has God forgotten to be merciful? Has he in anger withheld his compassion?" (77:7-9). This Israelite spoke from the depths of his wounded soul, "God, where are you!?" He was emotionally wrought and let his complaint be known to God. Instead of suppressing his anger and pain, he expressed it openly and directly. Christian victims who carry suppressed anger at God must be encouraged to go before Him and openly say what they feel. While maintaining respect and honor, victims need to express what is going on inside, even if their feelings are based on a lie. They need to get it out where they can tell God what they may have been suppressing for years.

I am a parent and at times must make decisions that frustrate and even anger my children. I am secure enough and love them sufficiently to encourage them to vent. As long as they show respect I want them to express their case, even with high emotion. After they are done I attempt to show them my perspective, while honoring their pain, lovingly helping them work through to understanding.

God is the perfect parent! Infinite in love and patience He can "take" an emotional torrent aimed at Him from a very finite, limited, yet greatly loved person. As emotions are expressed He honors them, moving in with compassion and care. He then through Scripture and the witness of the Holy Spirit reminds us of His perfect perspective. Like Job, victims are schooled in His sovereignty and justice, and like the writer of Psalm 77 encouraged to meditate on His past deeds. This emotional cleansing allows room for peace and inner healing to enter.

I will never forget preaching on this subject in a small church in the western United States. As I spoke of victimization that left faithful Christians secretly angry at God, a woman began to cry out loudly and uncontrollably. I felt led to encourage her to let it out, let her case be heard.

This young woman kept repeating "Where were You God; where were You?" Brought to the front, the congregation prayed as she unleashed a flood of emotion suppressed for years. Violated as a teenager, she felt let down by God, abandoned to carry her shame as a daily reminder of being abused.

How tenderly the Holy Spirit moved in as her anger poured out. Words of understanding, comfort, and love were spoken by those around her, obviously empowered of God. Over a forty-five-minute period she unleashed pent up, misdirected anger, opening the way for full healing. God did not pour wrath on her for expressing these feelings. He unleashed waves of love that not only washed away the lies Satan planted regarding God's abandonment, but cleansed the shame of victimization as well.

Pretending does harm to emotional well-being. The people of God must allow the hidden to be made known. In the light, destructive lies are disarmed, and the tender touch of God brings a transformation built on trust and based on truth. If you are angry at God, take your case before Him! It will open the way to a transforming encounter with the God of infinite love!

## 3. *Forgive "As We Forgive Our Debtors"*

Previously, I shared how the Lord brought me to understand that my deep depression, fear, and obsessive-compulsive thinking were symptoms of deeper woundings. Once convinced of this I did two things: First, I immediately made preparations to go to Colorado Springs for inpatient help. I knew the symptoms were quite serious, so going it alone was out of the question. The anointing and guidance of the Rapha staff at Cedar Springs Psychiatric Hospital were powerfully used to peel away my layers of defense.

Secondly, in the days before arriving in Colorado I asked the Holy Spirit to bring to my memory any and all events that were root causes to my dysfunction. What woundings had occurred in my past that were locked in the inner recesses of my memory, still affecting my behavior and emotions?

Because of my mental state, I was already spending long hours in solitude. The Holy Spirit invaded that time and began to gently bring to my mind memories of past woundings. It was, I must admit, a painful time. I did not realize how much I had "stuffed." Like many others I had thrown a blanket of forgiveness over my past—in part because I was instructed that it was the correct thing to do, in part because I did not want to deal with it. Remember, I hated pain and ran from it whenever possible!

As the Holy Spirit placed His finger on unresolved issues I wrote them down on a tablet. Within several days the list became quite long, covering my life up to that point. It was easy to see that there were two categories of unresolved issues:

The first were woundings that occurred to me. Most were from my childhood and adolescence, though not all. Some were more painful to recall than others, some direct assaults with intention to hurt, others unintentional abuses from people who really did not know better. This category of hurts will be the immediate focus of this section.

The second were hurts that I had inflicted upon others. That will be the focus of the next section of this chapter.

Over a period of time, the Lord led me to bring before Him each event. The process usually began with remembering what happened in some detail. At times my wife or a counselor was with me, so I would describe what I remembered. Invariably, as this unfolded before God's presence, pent-up emotions would begin to flow. At times there was weeping, other times anger over the violation. Because of the high emotion connected with these memories, I knew the issues were real and the wounds still there.

Regardless of the length of time in unleashing the emotions before God, on the other end was a singular requirement necessary. Time after time, event by event, regardless of severity or intent, the Lord would call me to extend forgiveness. It is the way of the Father, taught and modeled by the Son and empowered of the Holy Spirit. At times I struggled with it, sinfully wanting a person to feel pain, or holding them prisoner in the bars of my own bitterness. But whenever my wrestling was replaced by resting the matter in God's hands, genuinely forgiving, healing would flow in. The Holy Spirit's touch was always gentle and freedom would result. In certain cases I could internally feel an oppression release as forgiveness was given.

You probably are wondering if I went to every person involved, brought up the issue, and then extended forgiveness. My answer may sound simplistic, but it was the way it unfolded in my life. Whatever the Holy Spirit instructed, through His Word, inner witness, or trusted counselor, that is what I did. In the case of those who unintentionally wounded me, I did not generally go to them. The Lord enabled me to see through His eyes, and release them. The memory might remain, but there is no pain now. Rather a compassion and understanding that could come only from above.

For other woundings, it was critical that reconciliation include godly confrontation. As I grew up at home my dad was physically present but emotionally very distant. This took a toll on me resulting in deep pain and dysfunction, some of which I am still working through. In God's moment, led sovereignly by the Spirit, a face-to-face, issue-by-issue meeting did occur. Because I had already dealt with this before the Lord, much of the pain and anger was already released. But, it was still risky and tough for both of us. God, as He so often does, had already been at work in Dad's heart. As I talked, I could see that this powerful man, hardened by forty years in the coal mines, was both soft and sorrowful. I will *never* forget that time of reconciliation. It was holy, and we were both deeply touched. I love my dad and know that he is a beautiful human being. I'm proud to be his son!

There have been other people who wounded me that I did not personally confront. I simply forgave them before the Lord. One such wounding provides a good example.

Briefly stated, I hold certain beliefs about the work of the Holy Spirit that are not shared by everyone. That's fine, for across the Church such disagreements occur. But there is a clear biblical path to addressing a conflict one brother may have with another: first, go to that brother and seek understanding and reconciliation; if that is insufficient, move on to include others. The goal is always unity on the essentials of faith and love for one another.

However, in my case there were several men, all Christian leaders, who chose to make our theological differences both a public and personal matter.

In all this, I was dishonest about my emotions. I told people that it was all in the hands of the Lord, and I felt no malice. Inside I was stifling great pain and anger, because the whole affair hurt deeply.

Over the next five years I went on, believing the matter was for the most part behind me. How wrong I was! During my season of recovery God put His finger right on this issue. He showed me that I was bitter, and it was making me defensive. Sitting on a bench in a canyon at Glen Eyrie, with a therapist at my side, I erupted. A flood of tears and hurt poured out as I admitted how I really felt. And, as with each case before, the Spirit brought comfort, understanding, and healing. On that bench I did something genuinely that I had not done before. I truly forgave in the name and power of Christ.

## 4. Go and Reconcile with Your Brother

Our Lord is very clear about a believer's responsibility if he or she ever offends another. That person is to go to the offended person, seek forgiveness and reconciliation, and offer restitution. In the sermon on the mount Jesus said:

*Therefore, if you are offering your gift at the altar and there remember that your brother has something against you, leave your gift there in front of the altar. First go and be reconciled to your brother; then come and offer your gift. (Matthew 5:23-24)*

In Luke 15, the parable of the prodigal son illustrates the requirement of repentance and confession of sin, as well as the beauty of reconciliation. Further on in Luke we have the wonderful story of Zacchaeus. Transformed by the love of Christ, he seeks reconciliation and makes restitution with any and all offended parties. Seeking forgiveness of God and others is unmistakably a requirement of a kingdom lifestyle. It is also another part of the process of inner healing.

As I mentioned, the Holy Spirit did more than bring to my mind woundings at the hands of others. There was also a very long list of events that involved offenses on my part. Partly rooted in dysfunction, partly in sinful habits, I had done things in my past that were injurious to people. The events were of no good to me either, only further infecting my emotional wounds.

At first, as the Spirit brought these events to mind I was puzzled. I had confessed my sins at the time of conversion and had since turned to the Advocate innumerable times for forgiveness. Were not these experiences forgotten as Scripture said, forgiven and cast as far as the east is from the west? What was it about these particular sins that seemed to be linked to my emotional turmoil? What relationship was there between these memories and my inner healing?

As I went before the Lord with these questions He showed me a common element in each memory. These issues each involved individuals that I had in some way sinned against. While I may have sought the Father's forgiveness through Christ Jesus, I had never gone to these people to confess and reconcile. Through the Holy Spirit's conviction, I knew that the path toward my emotional wholeness must go by way of these people. Truthfully, it was probably the most frightening part of the journey; undoubtedly because of pride. But, in the strength of the Lord I stepped forth.

Most of the issues involved those closest to me— sins against my parents, sister, wife, children, and friends. Others were linked to co-workers and people from my past. In some cases the people involved knew and remembered the offense. In other cases what I had done was unknown by those I offended, making the situation tense at times, yet clearly guided of the Lord.

One issue did not involve people I knew, but a company. Once, while connecting our antenna to the back of the television I noticed a cable. Attaching it, I found that it increased our reception from three to eight stations. I thought little about it and just enjoyed the additional access. The Holy Spirit brought this up, convicting me deeply that it was in fact stealing.

Quickly I disconnected the cable. However, the Lord wanted more. With my wife I traveled to the company office, confessed my sin to the staff and asked forgiveness. I then paid double for the time period under question. I mention this embarrassingly, yet thankful for the tough lesson. Sin hurts! It hurts both the offender and the offended.

In the Lord's prayer we are taught to both extend forgiveness and seek the same of others (Matthew 6:12). It is unquestionable that many in the torment of depression, fear, bitterness, anger, and countless other dysfunctions are suffering because of an inadequate understanding and practice of this kingdom standard. For those truly seeking emotional healing, they too must pass by this way.

*Chapter Four*

# God-Given Longings
# and Satan's Lies

What are your deepest long-ings, those upon which all other personal desires are built? Maybe your mind rushed quickly to thoughts of landing your dream job, falling in love with the ideal person, being a recognized religious, political or show business per-sonality or getting away to an isolated spot where you could rest and recuperate. But I am talking about your *deepest* longings, not your surface desires.

I am not dismissing such desires as insignificant—they aren't. But I want you to push deeper still, to find the bedrock longings upon which such dreams rest. I would agree that while specific dreams or desires may vary, human longings are constant, person to person. My conviction is that longings are divinely endowed in human beings, not some chance set of emotions resulting from an "evolutionary process."

When God created Adam and Eve He placed within them certain undeniable longings meant to be fulfilled in Him, with Him and through Him. Such longings include:

- Fellowship with God.
- A secure and safe environment.
- A sense of worth.
- A desire to be unique and special.
- To be important.
- To be loved and love.
- To be enjoyed and enjoy.
- To find fulfillment and meaning in life.

As Adam and Eve remained in fellowship with their Maker, they experienced perfect harmony with Him, with each other and with creation. This harmony translated into physical, spiritual, emotional, and relational wholeness. Resting in their Creator, Adam and Eve felt fulfilled in all aspects of life. Their deepest longings were met. God gave Adam and Eve a unique place in His creation, placing them above all else, giving them dominion and responsibility. This contributed to a healthy and balanced self-esteem, as well as that wonderful vulnerability that enhanced love, enjoyment, and relational harmony. God-given longings were met in direct relationship to the One who instilled them in human beings in the first place. It was paradise.

But then, most tragically, comes the fall. Genesis 3

describes how Adam and Eve were convinced that their deepest longings could be met apart from fellowship with God. Satan deceived Eve, enticing her with the promise of fulfillment in every area of her life with no need for or reference to the Creator. Adam listened to Eve and they fed on this lie and swallowed its hollow promise that they would be equal to God rather than dependent upon Him. Adam and Eve's sin resulted in disharmony and brokenness, separation and death.

Here lies one of the great dilemmas of the fall. Disobedience separated God from humankind, but it did not eliminate the longings He placed within us! Though sin alienates people from God, they still long to know Him; to be safe and secure; to have a sense of worth; to be found unique and special; to be important; to experience the give and take of love; to enjoy others and be enjoyed; to find fulfillment and meaning in what they do. The longings are still there, present in every human being who has ever taken a breath. Oh, the tragedy—God-given longings within a race separated from the Source of fulfillment!

The question, of course, is "what can be done about this?" In comes Satan seeking to further deceive and ultimately destroy humankind. In a world alienated from God, Satan entices people to fulfill their God-given longings in totally ungodly ways:

- Idolatry is substituted for fellowship with God.
- Money and power are thought to bring security and safety.

- Personal performance is linked to self-worth.
- Approval replaces uniqueness.
- Position now determines importance.
- Sexual activity is substituted for genuine love.
- Godless pleasure is thought to bring lasting enjoyment.
- Career advancement is pushed as the answer to fulfillment in life.

Of course, any one of these propositions is a lie, each feeding the next and the human race is caught in a never-ending cycle of destruction.

With full commitment and resolve people pour their energies into the godless pursuit of these deep inner longings. But of course, apart from God, not one desire is ultimately met. Instead, after being worn out trying, broken spiritually and emotionally, dysfunction results. Rooted in the anger and rage of a meaningless existence, people become trapped in the perversions of abuse, molestation, sexual addictions, chemical dependence, and all other fruits of unrighteousness. Now the victim victimizes others and the cycle goes on. In generation after generation sin begets sin, the wounded go on to wound, the victim turns on others to hand down the legacy of pain. Apart from God, human longings remain unmet. The ultimate reward of this ungodly pursuit of God-given longings is brokenness.

Any one of a million examples could serve to illustrate this point. Let me tell you about Cathy. Today she is an adult recovering from sexual addiction. By the grace of God and the unsearchable riches of Christ she is experiencing healing. But how did she end up sexually promiscuous and chemically addicted in the first place?

## Not above Emotional Problems

Cathy was born into a typical American family. From all external appearances it was stable, but internally there were serious problems. I might add that Cathy's parents were Christians, faithful in church attendance and active in local church work. I point this out to emphasize that becoming a Christian does not automatically place people above emotional problems.

Like every child, Cathy had innate God-given longings. She needed the safety and security of nurturing parents, and the ongoing affirmation that builds self-esteem and worth. Cathy longed to be special, unique and capable of experiencing the fullness of unconditional love. These longings were meant to be rooted in God, taught, nurtured, and modeled by her parents. However, Cathy's parents were dysfunctional. Most people would not have recognized their actions as problematic. In fact, in both secular and church circles, their priorities were applauded. More than acceptable, they were rewarded.

Cathy's father was a workaholic. He spent long hours at his job in an effort to climb the corporate ladder. His actions were justified as "providing for his family and their future." The truth is, her father was suffering from a wounded self-image, seeking to gain worth and affirmation through his performance. It wasn't money that drove Cathy's father, it was dysfunction. The accolades of peers made him feel good about himself, so he worked all the more to have this longing met.

Cathy's mom was not a bad parent by the world's standards. In fact she was what some would see as the perfect model—active in Sunday school, fully committed to the PTA, Girl Scouts, and the AWANA program at church. If something needed to be done, Cathy's mother was the one to ask. Every pastor longs for a dozen more just like her.

The truth is, she was an addicted people pleaser. Fearing rejection, Cathy's mother did virtually anything and everything asked of her. She could not say no. She feared displeasing people in any way. Why? Because the wounds of her past drove her. Having felt rejection as a child, she did anything necessary to avoid feeling that pain ever again.

Two parents that any secular organization or local church would "kill for" were, over time, investing in their daughter's destruction. You see, while these parents were out seeking to secure and protect their own identities, they failed to nurture Cathy's. Dad was seldom home, which took a great toll on Cathy during adolescence. Mom was so busy pleasing everyone else, she forgot to give the necessary attention to Cathy as she developed into a young woman. Cathy longed to be treated as a special, uniquely loved and enjoyed person. She desired the intimacy that can develop with a father who expresses love and affection openly. And from her mother, Cathy needed a listening ear and confidant to guide her through the emotional upheaval of adolescence. But Cathy found neither from her parents.

Longings are very powerful, often sending people

on a desperate search for fulfillment. Cathy was a physically attractive and mature teenager. This brought a great deal of attention from boys in her high school. To Cathy it felt good, meeting a need in her life. Soon however, her longing to be special led to sexual activity. It was a false intimacy that caught her in a destructive cycle. Wanting to be desirable and accepted she gave in to sexual promiscuity, even though it left her with feelings of guilt and shame. This in turn ignited her longing to be found special and unique, leading to yet another relationship. The hunger for desirability led to sexual promiscuity, which once again brought feelings of shame and guilt.

As she grew into adulthood, Cathy began using drugs to silence the pain of her shame and guilt. This simply added to the never-ending cycle of destruction. The generational pursuit of fulfillment of God-given longings in ungodly ways continued. Satan's deceptive trap had ensnared yet another victim.

Cathy's story is an all-too-familiar one. In virtually every home the ravages of sin can be found. Life apart from God leads only to death. The very longings He placed within human beings drive people to self-destruct, while at the same time plant the seed of dysfunction in the next generation.

## Salvation through Jesus Christ

Into the horrible darkness of sin's far-reaching night came a glorious and powerful light. God, the one offended by the fall and by all rights justified to leave this race in the downward spiral of destruction, sent

His Son to break the power of evil. He came offering human beings full restoration to their pre-fall intimacy with God. Upon the cross of Calvary God's own Son bore in His flesh the curse of the fall. His shed blood was both payment for sin and full redemption from the clutches of evil to all who believe. There Jesus canceled the debt against human beings and placed under His feet the power of evil bent on destroying the human race (Colossians 2:13-15).

God did this out of love and gives to every believer new life in Christ. The emphasis here is upon the word "gives." There is absolutely nothing anyone could do to earn or deserve any aspect of so wonderful a salvation. Paul said it well in Ephesians 2:

> *As for you, you were dead in your transgressions and sins, in which you used to live when you followed the ways of this world and of the ruler of the kingdom of the air, the spirit who is now at work in those who are disobedient. All of us also lived among them at one time, gratifying the cravings of our sinful nature and following its desires and thoughts. Like the rest, we were by nature objects of wrath. But because of his great love for us, God, who is rich in mercy, made us alive with Christ even when we were dead in transgressions—it is by grace you have been saved. And God raised us up with Christ and seated us with him in the heavenly realms in Christ Jesus, in order that in the coming ages he might show the incomparable riches of his grace, expressed in his kindness to us in Christ Jesus. For it is by grace you have been saved,*

*through faith—and this not from yourselves, it is*
*the gift of God—not by works, so that no one can*
*boast. (2:1-9)*

In this passage, and elsewhere in his writings, Paul
emphasizes the great love and grace expressed to
people in Christ Jesus. The riches of this love and
grace are actually unsearchable, surpassing human
comprehension. To all who repent of their sin (which
is in fact seeking the fulfillment of God-given longings in ungodly ways), God offers forgiveness and a
transformed life! This new birth includes reconciliation with God through Christ and eternal life. It is
now possible to:

- Receive healing from all emotional wounds.
- Receive the fulfillment of one's deepest longings—in God, with God, and through God.
- Receive an entirely new identity rooted in the
  righteousness of Christ Jesus.

Author Neil Anderson has impacted countless
wounded people by identifying the true meaning and
scope of this new life in Christ. His works, *Victory Over*
*Darkness*, *The Bondage Breaker* and *Walking Through the*
*Darkness* are must reading for anyone caught in the
bondage of brokenness. Especially valuable is
Anderson's discussion of the believer's true identity
since receiving Jesus Christ. He has collected a list of "I
Am" statements which highlight the fulfillment of
God-given longings through Jesus. Dr. Anderson rein-
forces the believer's renewed significance, acceptance

and security by identifying Scriptures which clearly teach these truths.[1] For example, Anderson lists Scriptures under headings, as follows:

### Significance
Matthew 5:13—I am the salt of the earth.
John 1:12—I am God's child.
1 Corinthians 3:16—I am God's temple.
Ephesians 2:10—I am God's workmanship.

### Acceptance
John 15:15—I am Christ's friend.
Romans 5:1—I have been justified.
Colossians 1:14—I have been redeemed and forgiven of all my sins.
Colossians 2:10—I am complete in Christ.

### Security
Romans 8:35—I cannot be separated from God's love.
Romans 8:1—I am free from condemnation.
Colossians 3:3—I am hidden with Christ in God.
1 John 5:1—The evil one cannot touch me.

These Scriptures are but a handful of those that reveal the truth about a Christian's new identity in Christ. At the moment of conversion a transformation takes place in the believer's spirit. Reconciled with

---

[1] Neil Anderson, *Walking Through the Darkness* (San Bernardino, CA: Here's Life Publishers, 1991), pp. 91-93.

God, an individual is able to receive spiritual, emotional, and physical healing. He or she can also experience, through the power of the Holy Spirit, the fulfillment of God-given longings, leading to emotional and spiritual well-being. All this and more through Christ! All this and more given freely by God. The fullness of salvation is His gift of grace. *No wonder it is called good news!*

## Satan Wars against Wholeness

While Satan has been defeated since Calvary, he and his legions of demonic spirits war against these truths. Their first offensive is aimed at keeping people in the dark, unaware of the good news of salvation. This is why evangelistic outreach is so critical. Every person must hear of this God-given gift of love that brings freedom.

Satan also wars against believers. While a person may have accepted Christ and been born again, the evil one works to keep that individual in bondage. Using direct assaults and the systemic evil within our society, the destroyer bombards believers with lies. He directs his blows at the weakest places in a person's life. He tempts in areas of a person's previous sin and addictions, and harasses where woundings have occurred in an individual's past. Because most Christians have limited understanding of the spiritual power available, they easily fall prey to his lies. Without full knowledge of the truth that is in Christ, believers are often held in chains. Satan lays hold of an aspect of the believer's life, like an emotional wounding, and keeps that person in bondage.

Though freedom is truly available in Christ Jesus, deception keeps the person prisoner in the deepest part of his or her life.

Robert McGee, therapist and author of *Search for Significance*, suggests that there are four foundational lies that keep Christians from experiencing emotional well-being. These lies are rooted in sin, feed on unaddressed wounds of the past, and keep people from the freedom already theirs in Christ. The four foundational lies are:

1. I must meet certain standards to feel good about myself.
2. I must be approved by certain others to feel good about myself.
3. Those who fail are unworthy of love and desire to be punished.
4. I am what I am; I cannot change; I am hopeless.

McGee believes that certain forms of mental illness, emotional problems, and dysfunctions of all types can be linked to one or more of these lies. An individual has been violated in some way because of sin, leaving a painful wound. Satan then constantly feeds one or more of these lies into the person's mind, which leads to destructive behavior. As long as the wound remains unhealed, the lie shapes behavior, and the believer is in bondage.

Freedom only comes when two things happen. First the wound must be brought into the light, exposed before God. As long as it remains hidden, the enemy has the power to use it to harass an individual. In the light, Satan's grip can be broken by the power of Christ's blood. Secondly, the truth of God's love, forgiveness, and acceptance must replace the lies in the mind of the believer. A person who once hid in shame because of some wounding must now declare the truth of God's Word regarding his or her new identity. While the process takes time and a wide variety of therapeutic and spiritual approaches, the process of healing boils down to these two dynamics.

In *Search for Significance*, Robert McGee has more than adequately addressed the relationship of these lies to mental health. I have little to add to the thorough work presented in his book. I do feel it valuable to further explain and reinforce the importance of recognizing these deceptions as they relate to past emotional woundings. In this chapter I will discuss the sinful way people seek to fulfill the God-given longing for worth through personal performance. In following chapters we will address the other lies, their ability to destroy a person's mental and emotional well being, and the healing power of Jesus Christ.

## *Performance and Self-Esteem*

Every person longs to enjoy self-worth, to be someone special. I am certainly no exception. As I have repeated so often, such longings are God-given, a natural part of being human. And so it was not at all unique that I longed to be someone noticed and appreciated by others. But it was a life-long pursuit to meet this longing through performance that ultimately led to my breakdown.

Let me say that my parents did a remarkable job of raising my sister and me in light of their own pasts. Both Mom and Dad came from severely dysfunctional backgrounds. Mom was orphaned by the time she was eight, leaving her with deep wounds brought on by abandonment. My father came from a broken home that included multiple addictions and violence. In spite of this, my parents raised Bonny and me in a relatively safe and loving environment.

But dysfunction breeds dysfunction, and so home was not without its problems. Ironically, though parenting is one of the most important responsibilities on earth, no training is required. And so, Mom was nineteen and Dad twenty when they first assumed their respective parenting roles. In the midst of a great many good things they did, there were some destructive behaviors that deeply affected us children. Be assured our parents never intentionally sought anything but our well being. However, unaddressed brokenness in their lives reached beyond to the next generation.

It is not my purpose to lay out every issue that was problematic. However, two approaches to parenting did harmfully shape my life and that of my sister. First, my dad did not show affection or involvement in our lives. As children needing that affirmation, Bonny and I tried pleasing Dad by our behaviors. Mom contributed to this problem by rewarding us with love and affection when we behaved or did well. At the same time she would distance and withhold intimacy if in some way we did not meet her expectations. Today, Bonny and I are middle-aged adults and are A-number one workaholics, always looking for the next achievement that will bring that special feeling of worth and significance.

I think back to my junior and senior high school days. I quickly perceived that there were "number ones" and "number twos." "Number ones" were those special people who got involved in student government, athletics, drama, and other high-profile activities. "Number twos" were, well, unnoticed. Subconsciously desperate for affirmation I put my energies into becoming a "number one." If I could achieve, advance, or be recognized I felt good about myself. If I failed, in some way did not measure up, I felt like a nobody.

I continued this pattern into college. Athletics, a resident assistantship, campus committees, academics all became forums for significance. The cycle was deadly for two obvious reasons. First, God was totally absent from my life. This meant a lifestyle and morality totally inconsistent with biblical truth. Secondly, significance through achievement is a never-ending trap. Your feelings of worth only last momentarily, for soon another goal stands before you, and the hectic pursuit begins again.

By the time my college days came to a close I was drained. Emotionally I struggled with anger and bitterness, seeking relief through acts of sin. My life was unsatisfying and deep within I felt broken. Rather than anticipating the beginning of a professional career, I felt frustrated and worn out. All that time trying to be a somebody, and still inside feeling insecure and lacking significance.

It was at this point that I surrendered my life to the
Lord Jesus. The good news of God's love and forgiveness penetrated my hardened heart. I was born again
and the whole world looked different. The Lord's
forgiveness was so cleansing and freeing! He filled
the void that was driving me toward burnout. Jesus
truly was my Redeemer.

I became active in an evangelical church for fellowship, discipling, and training. And, believe it or not, I
soon found out that the church also had its system of
"number ones" and "number twos." Worth and significance was linked to performance just as it was in
the secular world. Clearly a person was saved by
grace, but it seemed that works and achievement
were the necessary ingredients for maturity.

Now there were two reasons to press on, work hard,
achieve and perform. First, it seemed from those in
leadership that this lifestyle pleased our Lord. Wanting His acceptance, I certainly desired to give my all
to Him. Secondly, the church linked worth to personal
achievement as much as the secular world. Christians
that really counted were those running hard in the
Lord's service. Winning people to Christ, leading
Bible studies, preparing for full-time Christian ministry—these activities were applauded and the people
doing them "special."

Still carrying the wounds of my past, I bought into
this dysfunctional behavior lock, stock, and barrel.
Don't get me wrong—I genuinely loved the Lord and
felt His Holy Spirit in my life. But with the determina-
tion of a workaholic I gave *my* all. As a young pastor
the word "no" was not in my vocabulary. I spent long

hours in pastoral ministry, while advancing through my master's and doctoral programs. Speaking engagements, church consultation, and denominational leadership all followed. By age thirty-two I held a seminary professorship; at thirty-four I was CEO of the seminary; by thirty-six I was creating graduate programs at a western college and planting a church. Simultaneously, I had authored two books and numerous articles with contracts for more in hand.

By this time serious signs of emotional upheaval were becoming evident. Fatigue, anxiety, and stress were constant companions. There were tensions in my relationship with Cheryl, because I was "busy in the Lord's work." Scriptural ideas like "denying myself," "carrying my cross," "not letting go of the plow," kept me going.

The Lord was good to me in spite of my dysfunctional workaholism. He graciously blessed my ministry and at times I enjoyed genuine and deep movements of the Spirit. But I was not at peace, always restless, wondering what else I should be doing for Him.

Near the time of my breakdown, the pace of my life was absurd. Deep within I grew angry, resented people who demanded my time, and withdrew more and more. Ultimately, my body could take it no longer and the cloud of darkness settled in upon me. Fear, anxiety, depression, and obsessive-compulsive thoughts overran my life. Now an eighteen-year quest in ministry to amount to something resulted in a personal nightmare. What went wrong?

For forty years I bought into the lie that worth and

significance were based on performance. It began in pre-adolescence, heightened in an educational system that promoted such ideals, and was propagated in the church as the true pathway to discipleship and maturity. Totally deceived, I bought the lie of Satan and it almost destroyed me; but for the grace of God, it could have cost me my family.

I have been a Christian long enough to know that I am not the only one ever bound by this deception. They may hold different jobs, live in a different context, or serve in a different church, but countless others are trapped just the same. When achievement and success occur, these people feel a sense of worth; when they fail the emotional torment is indescribable. People caught in this pattern fight rage, depression, pride, and fear. They grab for position and power, believing that somehow it makes them something special. This entire performance trap is a lie of Satan, deceiving Christians and non-Christians alike. It is an ungodly pursuit to fulfill a God-given longing that leads only to death.

The longing for worth and significance is met in only one way. By God's grace, all who accept Christ are given a new identity. It is a gift, impossible to earn and never deserved. Jesus provides every believer with full standing before God. The Bible refers to Christians as saints, adopted children, heirs of righteousness, complete in Jesus. There are no "number ones" and "number twos" in God's family. From the newest believer to the oldest saint, from the most famous Christian leader to the janitor of the country's smallest congregation—all are "number ones." Why?

Because standing in Christ is based solely on Him, nothing else!

Let me suggest what this means practically:

- God treasures you far more for who you are in Christ than what you could ever do for Him.
- God intends for Christians to enter His rest, not burn out in pursuit of significance.
- We are to obediently serve in the ways *He* calls us, trusting in His strength alone, not our own.
- We are free to fail, not fearing God's rejection. Even if we sin, repentance immediately restores full fellowship.
- We must learn to say NO! While we all are called to serve somehow, somewhere, we are not obligated to serve in every way everywhere.
- We can receive inner healing from the wounds that set us on such a destructive course in the first place.
- We must renew our minds, rejecting the lies of Satan, replacing them with the truth of God's Word that says we are loved, unique, special and significant through Christ Jesus our Lord!

I can never go back now that the Lord has healed my damaged emotions and set my feet firmly on Him, the Rock. He and He alone meets the longings in my life. Times of rest, silence and solitude in His presence have empowered me far more than performance ever did. I look back at the past years of service with mixed feelings. I'm grateful that God graciously blessed my ministry. At the same time I know much of what I did was wood, hay, and stubble! As I look ahead I thank God for a new perspective on life in Him. As difficult as that personal wilderness was, He brought me out with riches three times over.

Oh, how great a love this is, that God in His mercy would invite me to enter His rest! Rest—what a beautiful word to a person such as I. And the miracle of this rest is that it overflows into a more powerful ministry than the long hours of performance could ever bring. I now understand. His yoke is easy. His burden is light.

*Chapter Five*

# I Need You to Approve
# of Me—Or Do I?

*I*n the 1970s a major television network created a situation comedy
that took a satirical look at daytime soap operas. The
program had little, if any, socially redeeming values.
However, in several episodes it did make an interesting commentary on a major emotional problem,
portrayed by the character named Burt. It seems that
he went through a phase where he was convinced that
he was invisible. This led him to irrational behavior
and ultimately he was encouraged to seek therapy.

When asked why Burt felt he was invisible, his
response was quite revealing. He said, "Whenever I
go into a room full of people, no one ever sees me. If
I stand by my friends, they don't realize I'm there.
Sometimes I say something, and no one even acknow-

ledges that I have spoken. I must be invisible."

While the goal of the sketch was satirical humor, it was in fact a critical commentary on a significant problem in our society: loneliness, that sense of being unwanted, unacceptable, unattached to any person or group in society. The results of relational isolation are feelings of insecurity, lack of love, and insignificance. While the lonely are fearfully hesitant to use the word, they feel rejected.

Craig Ellison, respected Christian psychologist and author, lists loneliness as one of the most significant problems faced by people of the twentieth century. Here we are on a planet of over 5.2 billion people, and yet millions are emotionally unstable from the ravages of loneliness.

It is important to recognize that a lonely person is not necessarily some recluse who has chosen to intentionally isolate from society. Some of the loneliest people on earth live in big cities, have families, work alongside other individuals, and even attend local churches. But the nature of their interrelationship with others seldom if ever goes beyond formality. The lonely experience virtually no intimate and vulnerable social intercourse. They always feel like they are on the outside of the group looking in while the people inside grow closer. There is that deep inner sense of being unwanted, unacceptable, unlovable.

It has been suggested that it is loneliness that makes the local bar so attractive to people. Certainly for some it is simply a place to drink oneself into a drunken stupor. But for many other people, the bar is a gathering of lonely hearts. A place where they go to experience a degree of acceptance and affirmation, as distorted as it may be. It fills that desperate need so many broken people have, aptly reflected in the theme song to a television program set in a local bar: "You want to go where everybody knows your name." This is the cry of the lonely and rejected in society. People long to have relationships with others, to be accepted, to feel that they belong at least somewhere.

## *According to God's Design*

We have already established two basic truths about the human race. First, we recognize that God created people with certain basic, yet critical, longings. He endows individuals with the innate desire to be unique and special. Every man, woman, and child longs to be valued, to love and be loved, to enjoy and be enjoyed. In addition there is a divinely endowed drive to be fulfilled and satisfied in what one does in life. These longings were placed in humans by their Creator, and for good reason.

God intended that all these longings would be born, nurtured, developed, and fulfilled as people intimately related to Him. United with their Creator, people could be whole, experiencing a beautiful harmony between God, one another and creation. This harmony also was to influence personal self-esteem as man and woman took their rightful place in creation.

In the last chapter we discussed the effects of the fall. Adam and Eve's sin gave birth to generation after generation of broken, sinful people. These longings, meant to draw individuals to God, now are driven by a sinful nature that leads to emotional, physical, and spiritual destruction.

Let's briefly look beyond the fall, as recorded in Scripture, to consider the nation of Israel. God through Abraham gave birth to a nation who would be His covenant people (Genesis 12). Purely out of mercy and grace, He established Israel as His own, promising to place the resources of heaven at their disposal. He covenanted to separate them as a holy people, make them a mighty nation, and give them a good land as their inheritance. There was one primary requirement for Israel in relationship to this covenant. They must walk in obedience to God, according to the laws laid down by Him, ultimately given to Moses. If they were faithful, the Lord promised to show love to a thousand generations of those who love Him and keep His commandments (Exodus 20:6).

If we look carefully at the Israelites we get a glimpse of God's plan for nurturing self-esteem and emotional well-being in this people. Notice that God related to the nation as a whole by way of representative leaders—the prophets and priests. Through them He communicated His love and acceptance to the entire nation. As a unified whole, the nation clearly knew it held a special place in the economy of God. Israel had  a strong identity as a separate people, holy unto God. This message of affirmation, acceptance, love, security, and unique destiny was then communicated from the nation to each tribe. Each tribe likewise further defined their uniqueness, communicating this message to each clan, the clan to the family, and ultimately by the family to the individual.

Think for a moment about the meaning of this to an individual Israelite child. He or she was not meant to live emotionally bewildered; God's intention was that this child be fully aware that he or she was special, unique in the world, fully loved and accepted, knowing full well his or her place in their family, clan, tribe, and nation. This message was communicated throughout the entire social structure of the Israelite nation. They were a covenant people, holy unto the Lord, and every single Israelite knew where he or she stood. They belonged!

Of course I emphasize this was God's intention. The Israelites, however, were led repeatedly to choose against God. They would rebel, sinning against God by embracing the ways of the wicked people around them. Ultimately such disobedience put their uniqueness and security at risk. Rather then being affirmed by God, during times of disobedience He would temporarily reject them. Now, the message communicated from nation to tribe to clan to family to individual was one of brokenness. Sin fractured the nation all the way down to the family unit. What resulted was bondage and captivity. This cycle is recorded all through the Old Testament. What went wrong?

It is the same problem that began at the fall and continues today. Any attempt to fulfill God-given longings in ungodly ways always ends in destruction and death—emotionally, physically, and spiritually.

## We Share a Common Fear

To one degree or another most people want to be

accepted and conversely fear any and all rejection. This desire for acceptance and fear of rejection significantly shapes how people relate to others and ultimately how they feel about themselves. It is particularly important that the people defined as "significant" in a person's life embrace and include that person in their world. If in any way a "significant other" sends a message of rejection, the pain is overwhelming. To be told you are unacceptable, unwanted, unlovable, or undesirable is a wounding people will do almost anything to avoid. It is most destructive when this message is sent during early childhood or adolescence. It can lead to deep emotional upheaval and unhealthy and dysfunctional ways of relating to people.

Mike Carter is a close personal friend and colleague in vocational Christian ministry. He also is a man just beginning to come to terms with a lifetime of pain stuffed deep inside, chronically bearing dysfunctional fruit. I see Mike quite often and my heart goes out to him. He is in his mid-forties, has twenty years of ministry behind him and is in the throes of an identity crisis. Mike knows God is bringing healing, but he also recognizes that it has been a tough time, with lots of tears along the way. He admits that, as important as it is to let the Holy Spirit reveal the truth, it is not pleasant to find out you have been living dysfunctionally. "It takes the strength of God alone," said Mike, "to be honest about yourself and the basis of your ministry at my age. Especially when you begin to see a lot of what you do and why you do it is wrong."

Mike Carter has spent his life trying to avoid disapproval. He just can't take the pain. He is a chronic people-pleaser and avoids confrontation at almost any price. Of his home life, Mike said it has the appearance of a peaceful environment. But, in his words, it is a very "deceptive peace." He avoids confronting or discussing any issues that would arouse conflict. And, Mike has sent a clear message that he expects the same of his wife and teenage children.

When discussing it I could not imagine it possible to actually live with three other people and not have open conflict. But Mike assured me it is not only possible, in his home it has been a requirement. Mike commented, "If I see something that bothers me in our home, I just ignore it." Likewise Mike has expected everyone to live in the same denial. What results is internal turmoil, but sweet smiles all around. He told me that by avoiding issues he avoided disapproval. Of course Mike now sees the deception of this lifestyle and is beginning to step out of the silence.

Mike and I also talked at length about his twenty years in pastoral ministry. Quite frankly I could not imagine a confrontation-free environment in that context. My experience has been that in one way or another it is a fairly regular occupational hazard. Mike agreed and admitted that his need for approval and fear of disapproval hurt him and his ministry over the years. For Mike, any form of personal rejection sent him into emotional upheaval. He particularly bottomed out when he was asked to leave his first pastorate after seven years. The dismissal was devastating, but he stifled the pain, put on a glad smile and moved on. Mike told me he would not even reflect on what went wrong there. He just entered denial and sought out another church.

Mike's second pastorate lasted a little over a decade. By even conservative standards it would not have qualified as an overly fruitful ministry. Mike described his approach to pastoral ministry as follows:

- He would do almost anything anyone asked.
- He was "Johnny on the spot" whenever anyone was in trouble.
- He never directly confronted potentially volatile issues.
- If change was necessary, he did not deal with it directly, but chose to influence or manipulate from some back door.
- He always tested to see which way the "wind" was blowing on an issue so as to be "politically" correct.
- If group tension ever did arise, Mike had one and only one goal—eliminate the tension so everyone could be happy.

After forty-five years, twenty in pastoral ministry, Mike Carter was burnt out. He just could not hold it all together anymore, with his church, his family, or himself. The emotional fabric of his life began to quickly unravel. And so, with no other choice, Mike left the ministry, moved to another town and began to seek God for help. He wasn't even sure of what was wrong or what to do. But Mike knew his people-pleasing, problem-denying days had to end before he was destroyed.

God mercifully placed his family in a perfect context for healing. They began to attend a grace-based church that encouraged an atmosphere of vulnerability. As the Holy Spirit gently pressed in, the Carter family began to open up and be honest. Though far from a picnic, it has been the right prescription for their healing. The Carters have risked breaking the silence, slowly trusting others with their hidden woundedness, seeking to uncover the destructive roots of such dysfunctional behavior.

Mike was visiting me recently, so I asked him if he could yet identify what was the root cause of his behavior. He probably felt safe with me knowing all about my own experience. As a result, he opened up and spoke at length about his father, his childhood, and his very painful adolescence. He wept several times as he rehearsed this history, evidence that he was still dealing with it. But through the tears he continually gave glory to God for the healing taking place in his life.

Mike first discussed his father, particularly their relationship during his early childhood and adolescence. He commented that he always felt insecure as a child, especially when he was with his father. Three memories stood out in Mike's mind. First, the day when at age five his dad said, "Mike, you're too old for me to kiss and hug. From now on we will just shake hands." Secondly, he recounted that whenever he would begin to share an idea with his dad, he would be cut off in mid-sentence. His dad would then tell Mike what was wrong with that notion. Thirdly, Mike remembers very little one-to-one time with his father. His dad worked a day job, then came home to work in the basement in a small cabinetmaking business.

Mike Carter, because of his intellect, was sent to first grade at four years of age. Reflecting back, he sees that while capable of performing at the level of other students, he was emotionally still four years old. Three things resulted. First, for twelve years, he never fit in with his classmates. Secondly, he was teased about his inability to play and perform on the playground at the level of his classmates. Thirdly, Mike was constantly sent home with notes to his parents that he did not conform to behavioral expectations. Vividly and with strong emotion, he told me about an incident that occurred in the first grade. The teacher was forming a little rhythm band and gave Mike a belt of bells to play. Rather than holding it in his hand to shake, he strapped it around his wrist. The teacher scolded him openly, citing it as an example of his non-conformist behavior.

Mike told me that he knows that these woundings led directly to his dysfunctional behavior. Mike said, "For my entire life I have been insecure around people, afraid of their disapproval. I have believed that there is something wrong with me. And in any discussion, I began by concluding that what the other person says will be right and I will be wrong."

Mike Carter is a classic example of a person

desperate for approval and fearful of rejection. These longings, distorted by emotional woundings in his childhood, resulted in very dysfunctional behavior. Today, by the grace of God, Mike is in a season of recovery. The Holy Spirit is bringing healing to those emotional wounds and at the same time teaching Mike the truth about his true identity in Christ. His behavior is changing as peace fills the place where upheaval and fear once resided.

## Dysfunctional Styles of Relating

People respond differently to the wounds of rejection and disapproval. They adopt one or more of several ways of relating to people. Regardless of the path they choose to follow, the goal is always the same. "What can I do to keep from facing rejection or feeling disapproval?"

Respected Christian therapist Matt Barnhill suggests that there are four primary ways people wounded like Mike respond relationally. First, there is the person who runs from intimacy. He or she may be very friendly on the surface, but they keep a physical and/or emotional distance from others. They never get vulnerable, allowing no one to get down to where he or she really lives. They do this to protect themselves from rejection. Fearing that intimacy will reveal their "true inferiority," they learn to live without meaningful relationships. That way, they will never experience the rejection they anticipate.

Other people cope with their woundedness by developing very irritating personalities. They relate to people with contempt and sarcasm, or are in a perpetual bad mood. They do this to create an environment that pushes people away if they get too close. Of course, this irritating person then blames those who chose to distance from them. By blaming, the responsibility for the relationship problem shifts from the wounded person to everyone else around them. This is a form of denial, allowing the individual to keep their wounds hidden, even from themselves.

A third way individuals with such problems choose to relate is by setting unrealistic expectations upon others. Their requirements in relationships are so high and so unreasonable that it would be impossible for anyone to ever meet them. But the wounded person believes that if someone genuinely loves them, they would meet their unrealistic expectations! The fact that they do not is proof positive that they really don't care. When others fail to come through as expected, the wounded person simply responds, "See, I knew you would reject me." In essence the wounded person is setting up a situation that *gets the rejection over with as soon as possible*. They do not allow themselves to consider not being rejected, because if in the end they were, it would be too painful to handle.

The most common dysfunction seen in people like Mike Carter is approval addiction. Here, the person adopts an approach to relationships based solely on one criteria: *What must I do to please them?* These individuals are so wounded by rejection that they will do whatever is expected to be approved of and belong. For some, this means adopting that sweet, kind, nice personality that everyone likes. They work hard to be energetic, helpful, are easy to get along with and pleasing. Of course the down side of this is that they can be easily dominated and manipulated by aggressive people. Also, even a moderately discerning person soon sees their actions as a mere facade, hiding a very wounded person inside.

Of course being nice is not the only option for the approval addict. Some groups don't accept nice people. They require other characteristics like rebellion, disrespect, aggressive behavior, immorality, and lawlessness. Many times teenagers, for example, will change their behavior and standards one hundred and eighty degrees to get into such groups. Parents become baffled and incensed at the look and demeanor of their son's or daughter's new friends. What's more, they see their child beginning a nasty metamorphosis before their very eyes, and they wonder why. While the root issue may yet be unclear, the bottom line is their child longs to belong. And, despite the unlovely look of this new crowd, it has become a place of acceptance and approval. An approval addict will do virtually anything to receive approval and escape rejection.

Recently, network television coverage was given to a teen sex scandal in southern California. A group of boys, calling themselves "The Posse," awarded points to club members for sexual encounters. The matter rocked the community at its moorings, leaving parents asking such questions as, "Why would my son want to be part of such a group? Why would my daughter allow herself to be used in such an immoral and dehumanizing way?" Certainly, at least in part, the pressure to belong, conform and be accepted was an aspect of the problem. And of course this incident, as with others discussed in this section, shows the hideous, destructive nature of sin.

Over time running from rejection and hiding that sense of inferiority takes its toll. No one can keep such a pretentious act up forever. Sooner or later the chase wears the individual out. More and more, despair and depression begin to surface. The approval addict grows angry and resentful at the constant control and manipulation brought on by dominant people in their lives. It is then that I believe they are ready to address the lie that motivates such dysfunctional behavior. And that deception is this: *If only I had the approval of others I would be okay.*

## Healing for Worth-through-Approval Seekers

There are three things that bring healing to people with this type of dysfunction:

1. First, as Christians, they must come to a greater knowledge of what is theirs in Christ Jesus. In Ephesians 3:8, Paul refers to the "unsearchable riches of Christ." The emphasis is upon the unbelievable and almost unfathomable gifts of grace bestowed upon believers through Christ Jesus. We receive in Christ a completely new identity. We have been reconciled to God the Father, drawn near by the blood of the Lord (Ephesians 2:13). Even more, believers are now a chosen people, unique, belonging to God, and set apart for a divinely ordained purpose (1 Peter 2:9ff). These promises of love, forgive-

ness, reconciliation, and restoration are repeated throughout the New Testament. Here, in the truths of redemption, lie our identity, worth, and belonging. These are the truths that can set the broken and rejected free from their perpetual pain.

2. Secondly, the dysfunctional must allow the Holy Spirit to bring healing to the wounds that are the root of their destructive behavior. This process has been thoroughly discussed in chapter two. Those who see the fruit of dysfunction and woundedness in their life need to allow the Holy Spirit to bring into the light that which was hidden in the dark. When they express the agony and pain of past abuse and violation before the Lord, the Spirit brings healing to their inner being. This healing is a gift of grace, provided by the atoning work of the Lord Jesus. Like sanctification, it is a sovereign process in which the individual cooperates with the Counselor's work of transformation.

3. Thirdly, as is true with inner healing in general, those moving on toward freedom must learn to battle the Deceiver. He is the prince of liars, bombarding people with untruth, hoping that they will act upon lies and yet again be held captive. In this particular case, the lie that will continue to harass is that "the approval of others in some way determines my self-

worth." For those previously held in bondage to this deceit, such constant thoughts can be overwhelming. Paul gave God-inspired guidance when he said:

*For though we live in the world, we do not wage war as the world does. The weapons we fight with are not weapons of the world. On the contrary, they have divine power to demolish strongholds. We demolish arguments and every pretension that sets itself up against the knowledge of God, and we take captive every thought to make it obedient to Christ. (2 Corinthians 10:3-5)*

Paul is revealing a critical principle of battle against the lies of Satan. First, the evil one primarily attacks us in the mind, filling our heads with lies. To overcome, all thoughts must be taken captive, subject to the truth of God's Word. Thus, when a person is compelled to act so as to please others, that person must stop and think. "Is this desire rooted in my previous need for approval, meant to give me a false sense of worth?" If it is, take the thought captive, declaring the truth of the believer's grace-given identity in Christ.

Our minds must be renewed, filled with truth in order to recognize and defeat the lies that once led to dysfunctional behavior (Romans 12:2). To accomplish that, I do two things. First, I carry a notebook filled with Scriptures that speak the truth regarding my identity in Christ. I have particularly included passages that relate directly to my past dysfunction. Secondly, in my pocket is a medallion given to me by the staff at Cedar Springs. On it are inscribed these words:

Because of Christ's redemption,
I am a new creation of infinite worth.
   I am deeply loved,
   I am completely forgiven,
   I am fully pleasing,
   I am totally accepted by God,
   I am absolutely complete in Christ.

These are the truths that can set all people free, regardless of past woundings, abuse, and dysfunction. As one who has been touched by such freedom, I can now say, "While I may desire your acceptance and approval, I no longer must have it to give me worth. I am a child of the Most High and I belong!"

*Chapter Six*

# The Fear of Failure

Tucked away in Job, a book often referred to but seldom read, is one of my favorite Scriptures: Job 38:7. What captivates me about this particular verse is the image it creates in the mind. It is a behind-the-scenes look at the glorious events of creation. The context is God's opening rebuttal to Job's lengthy discourses regarding his undeserved lot in life. The Lord begins by instructing Job about his finite and limited perspective on reality. To emphasize these points, God poses a series of questions to Job that place matters in their proper perspective.

In chapter 40, after setting forth a lengthy list of profound questions the Lord says to Job, "Will the one who contends with the Almighty correct him? Let him who accuses God answer him!" To this Job, now properly put in his place, responds, "I am unworthy—how can I reply to you?"

In the beginning verses of God's rebuke He asks the following of Job:

> *Where were you when I laid the earth's*
>      *foundation?*
>  *Tell me, if you understand.*
> *Who marked off its dimensions? Surely you*
>      *know.*
>  *Who stretched a measuring line across it?*
> *On what were its footings set,*
>  *or who laid its cornerstone—*
> *while the morning stars sang together*
> *and all the angels shouted for joy?*
>      *(Job 38:4-7)*

Each time I reread verse seven I am overcome with wonder and awe. Consider, even visualize, what this Scripture is portraying. The angelic host and celestial beings were overwhelmed watching God reveal His power and glory while creating the universe. Even though they continually behold God in all His magnificence, seeing Him speak forth creation was too much to leave them just sitting in silence. As God acted, the celestial beings broke forth in song and the angelic host shouted, filled to overflowing with joy in what they beheld. They could not contain themselves at this omnipotent display of God. The angels of heaven were emotionally overcome! They had to shout and sing, watching as God called forth such a beautiful "something" out of nothing.

By reading the first two chapters of Genesis, it is

easy to see that angels were not the only ones emotionally engaged in creation. God was also delighted! Five times in chapter 1 God looked at what He had done and pronounced "it was good!" Far from passive and emotionally stoic about what He was creating, God was engaged and well-pleased. The work of His spoken words satisfied Him greatly. The sixth time He reflects upon the created order, God goes beyond stating that it was good. He says it was *very* good!

The reader cannot help but see that our heavenly Father took pleasure and expressed satisfaction in what He did. His creation was magnificent, breathtaking, awe-inspiring, and exciting. It was to all the residents of heaven a wonderful work, inspiring songs, and shouts of praises to the Almighty.

Let me risk redundancy by restating this key point. God took pleasure in what He did in creation. It delighted Him very much, satisfying God as right and good. But at the same time we recognize that the work of creation did not give God any additional worth, significance, or self-esteem. Every aspect of God's nature is rooted in His eternal, infinite, and holy self-existence. In other words, He did not root His identity *within* what He did! But what God did in creation certainly *reflected* His identity! Look at this vast and beautiful universe and one properly discerns the perfect, pure, purposeful, ordered, infinite, and eternal characteristics of the Creator (Romans 1:20; Psalm 19). In simple terms, what God does reflects who He is. But keep in mind that what He does never determines who He is!

The Bible tells us that human beings were created in His image (Genesis 1:26-27). Through finite incapacity, men and women were made to reflect the nature and character of God. While there is a great deal that can be said about this truth, in this context I want to highlight two important points. First, God intended that human beings be secure in their identity apart from what they do. God gave men and women worth, uniqueness, importance, and a sense of being special. Secure in their relationship with God, men and women were meant to experience fellowship with Him, and enjoy intimacy and genuine love one to another.

But secondly, God intended for people to take delight and find satisfaction in what they did. As Adam and Eve put their hands to the task before them, they would find personal satisfaction and fulfillment. I am convinced that God intended them to feel emotionally inspired and positive as they fulfilled the cultural mandate of Genesis 1:28:

> God blessed them and said to them, "Be fruitful and increase in number; fill the earth and subdue it. Rule over the fish of the sea and the birds of the air and over every living creature that moves on the ground."

Prior to the fall, the call to have dominion over the earth was intended to be a source of great satisfaction for humankind. Like God, Adam and Eve were meant to enjoy the responsibilities placed before them. Again, as with Him, the works of their hands were to reflect their identity, mirror their esteemed place in all creation. But also, as with the Father, what Adam and Eve did was never intended to give them uniqueness or importance, but simply to reflect it.

And so, as emphasized numerous times throughout this book, human beings were given significance and uniqueness by God, experienced security and belonging with God, and found satisfaction and succession in what they did through God. This was the wonderful plan of God for generation upon generation after Adam and Eve.

But as we have seen before, we come face to face with the effects of the fall. Deceived by Satan, Adam and Eve disobey God's requirement regarding the tree of the knowledge of good and evil. Deciding against God, Adam and Eve now act on their own and the result is far from satisfying and successful. The "work of their hands" resulted in wrong, brokenness, and failure. Immediately recognizing their transgression, Adam and Eve ran and hid. Why? Because they knew that they had failed, and anticipated the Father's blame and punishment. They looked at what they had done and saw that it was bad, very bad.

Previously we discussed the devastating consequences of the fall on human beings. Separated from God, people are unable to find true significance, importance, belonging, love, and affirmation. Satan only leads humans in a mad chase to find fulfillment of these longings in ungodly, destructive ways.

## No Fulfillment or Satisfaction

But in this chapter I want to emphasize one consequence of the fall that devastates the entire race. Apart from God, people no longer consistently experience fulfillment and satisfaction in what they do. Instead men, women, and children quite often fall short; they fail. And rather than experiencing delight and inspiration, people feel the frustration and despair of not measuring up!

Notice how Satan ensnares people in ongoing dysfunction and ultimate destruction. First, he convinces individuals that they can find significance and worth apart from God particularly through performance and the approval of others. Satan knows full well that such substitutes will never meet the deepest longings of the human heart. He also knows that apart from God it is impossible to consistently perform and relate successfully. People will fail! As they do, using anyone and every way he can, the evil one oppresses people with this devastating message, "You are a failure! You are unworthy of love and deserve to be punished!"

For millions of people the fear of failure is a deep hidden pain that births any of a variety of dysfunctional responses. Men, women, and children have been seriously wounded in the past when significant others have reacted to their failures, serving as the mouthpiece of Satan by cursing them with Satan's lies. "To fail makes you a failure. And everyone knows failures deserve nothing but blame and punishment." For those haunted by this emotional wounding, there seems to be only one recourse. If at all possible stay in hiding!

But thankfully Satan does not have the final word

to those who fall short! God does, and His word to the broken and lost is good news. It is very good and linked to the gracious, merciful work of His Son, Jesus Christ, on behalf of all who have ever failed. Later in this chapter we will look more directly at this redeeming work that will once again set morning stars to singing and angels to shouting!

## God's Attitude Regarding Children

Children hold a special place in the economy of God. The Bible is full of references regarding their preferred and protected status. They are to be dedicated unto the Lord, trained in the way of wisdom and taught the story of God's redemptive history (Proverbs 22:3; Joshua 4:6). Children were created to give praises unto the Lord, capable of routing the enemies of God and silencing the avenger (Psalm 8:2). Jesus commanded that little ones be brought to Him for blessing and confirmed their unique status in the kingdom of God. He even encouraged adults to be childlike if they hoped to enter God's eternal realm (Luke 18:15-17). And unquestionably, one of the sternest rebukes in all of God's Word comes in reference to children.

> *At that time the disciples came to Jesus and asked, "Who is the greatest in the kingdom of heaven?"*
> *He called a little child and had him stand among them. And he said: "I tell you the truth, unless you change and become like little children, you will never enter the kingdom of heaven. Therefore, whoever humbles himself like this child is the*

> *greatest in the kingdom of heaven.*
> *"And whoever welcomes a little child like this in*
> *my name welcomes me. But if anyone causes one of*
> *these little ones who believe in me to sin, it would*
> *be better for him to have a large millstone hung*
> *around his neck and to be drowned in the depths of*
> *the sea." (Matthew 18:1-6)*

In addition, clear instructions are given to fathers regarding child-rearing, warning them not to plant seeds of bitterness that would lead to discouragement (Colossians 4:21).

God looks upon childhood and adolescence as a critical period in human development. He intends that parents act responsibly, according to scriptural mandates, laying the foundation of a God-related identity within the child. John Trent and Gary Smalley, in their book *The Blessing*, believe that a biblical pattern of building such self-esteem includes five basic elements:

> The meaningful touch.
> A spoken message.
> Attaching "high value" to the one being blessed.
> Picturing a special future for the one being blessed.
> An active commitment to fullfilling the blessing.[1]

---

[1] Gary Smalley and John Trent, *The Blessing* (Nashville: Thomas Nelson Publishers, 1986), p. 24.

Over and over again parents are to send these messages to their children, leaving no question about their identity and worth before God. When mothers and fathers accept this responsibility, empowered by the Holy Spirit, children grow into emotionally healthy adults, escaping the wounds and lies of the evil one that bring bondage and dysfunction. Secure in their God-given uniqueness and worth, they are free to enjoy intimacy, love, and satisfaction in their calling. Performance, approval, and the fear of failure will not ensnare them in the destructive behaviors so common to many.

## Failure and Painful Memories

It is important that we keep before ourselves God's ideal and the helpful insights of men like Trent and Smalley. But if anyone ever hopes to be set upon the right path, he or she must take an honest look at what is really happening in families today. As adults, few of us can look back at our childhood and relate to God's intended plan for human development. Our experiences are far too dissimilar. If healing is to come, and be passed on to the next generation, we must face the wounds of our own childhoods and seasons of adolescence. Only after identifying our own victimization and receiving Christ's inner healing will we be free to fulfill our responsibilities to our children and our children's children.

What is really happening or has happened to children—including ourselves? Parents, suffering from various types and degrees of dysfunction have or are now wounding their children. Buying into

Satan's lies, propagated throughout our world system, parents are notorious for communicating messages like those already discussed. "Performance determines self-worth and self-esteem. Approval is necessary to feel good about oneself. Fail and you are a failure, deserving of blame and punishment." These were the lessons countless children were taught, and thus as adults they pass them on like a contaminated inheritance.

I want to briefly share four stories that highlight this pattern, with particular emphasis upon the paralyzing fear of failure. I do so emphasizing that while the incidents are each unique, they share several common destructive elements. Each account was communicated during a counseling session from individuals struggling with the many fruits born from the fear of failure.

When Jenny was a child of twelve, she already had responsibilities beyond her age. Jenny's parents both worked, leaving her to babysit her two younger brothers. In addition, her duties included washing, ironing, and other domestic chores. In effect, Jenny was required to assume parental responsibilities, though herself a child.

Jenny's father was aggressive, and her mother very submissive and docile. If things at home were not found as expected, he would fly into a rage. On one occasion he came home to find that Jenny had not completed the chores. Confronting her, Jenny retorted with a sarcastic remark. Immediately her father struck Jenny, knocking her to the floor. In describing this Jenny said, "I literally saw stars after he hit me." When I asked how she felt about her father's actions she said, "I'm sure it was my fault, I should have done what he said in the first place."

Darren Glasser's father was a strong, domineering, aggressive man. His height and build were impressive and his demeanor intense. He was an athletic man, and would regularly play various sports with Darren and his brothers. But Dad consistently sent a clear message to all his boys. He could beat them at any sport they ever tried. Dad always won, always gloated in the victory, and continually reinforced the fact that "they lost."

On one occasion, while playing basketball, Darren grew frustrated at his dad's aggressive play. He walked off the court in anger, speaking an obscenity directed at his father. His dad, reacting more like a teenager than an adult, told Darren, "Any time you think you can take me, just say the word."

Fourteen-year-old Darren went to his bedroom and the anger continued to build. Overcome by it, he shouted to his dad out the window, "I'm ready whenever you want." To that Darren's dad came to his bedroom and proceeded to beat up his son. Overpowered and lying on the floor in great pain, Darren was doubly defeated—first by the fight, and secondly by hearing yet again his father's often repeated statement, "You couldn't beat me at anything!" Darren ended the story by saying, "I should have never said what I did."

Josh Bergstrom was reared in a home where performance determined worth, and failure brought on shame. Grades were commonly used to measure success and failure in his home, particularly by his mother. Repeatedly, as report cards came home, he would face a multi-faceted scolding when his mother's expectations were unmet. Comparisons were made between him and well-known failures in the community. Constantly the statement, "You won't amount to anything," was used as a whip to enhance performance.

Josh came to me suffering from all the dysfunctions relating to workaholism. While recounting the stories of this repeated pattern, he grew tense and emotional. He told me that for some reason one incident stood out in his memory with particular pain. I was amazed at the degree to which he detailed this prominent scolding. He remembered the grade, subject, teacher, where he was standing, and who was there. Most of all he remembered what his mother said when she saw the D he received in history. Her response: "All you have is horse - - - - between your ears. You might as well quit school, because you'll amount to nothing." It was twenty-seven years later when asked how he felt about himself, Josh said, "Deep inside I'm afraid that I really am a nothing."

I grew up in a neighborhood full of kids, all products of the baby boom. We never had a problem finding someone to play with, regardless of the game or activity. In our neighborhood lived a boy named Jimmy Evans. He was about my age, and I can't remember a time when I didn't know him. To this day I often see him when I travel home for a visit. Though Jimmy has moved to another state, his parents, like mine, still live in the same neighborhood.

All these years Jimmy has reflected a very insecure persona. Shy around people, he lacks confidence and is quick to use humor to disarm attention aimed at himself. Not too long ago I had the occasion to counsel Jimmy's sister. She was dealing with anger, and the trail ultimately led back to her dad.

While sharing her own story, Carol told me of an incident involving Jimmy that spoke volumes. It seems her dad was intimidating and quite stern at home. Each of the children dealt with this in different ways. For Jimmy, his father's behavior left him very nervous and insecure. In addition, Jimmy had a problem with bed-wetting into early adolescence. This often infuriated Jimmy's dad. He would try to get him to stop by belittling, shaming, and other abusive behavior. On one occasion, upon Jimmy's wetting the bed, Jimmy's father made him go outside and stand naked, while his mother stripped the bed. Carol said he wept in humiliation as their father ranted and raved about his son, "the baby."

As Carol shared this story, my heart broke for Jimmy. How devastating to be treated in such an inhumane way. Instead of understanding and compassion, Jimmy was shamed and made to feel a failure. Locked inside this forty-year-old man is a little boy that feels as though he never measured up. Is it any wonder that Jimmy is insecure?

These are but four of hundreds upon hundreds of such accounts that illustrate the intense woundings that affect a person's behavior long into adulthood. In point of fact these incidents represent the twentieth-century antithesis to the biblical blessing identified by

Trent and Smalley. You will notice that each account shares three common ingredients. First, each of the children in some way failed to meet a parent's expectation. Secondly, they were severely, even abusively punished as a result of this failure. Thirdly, they were told by word or deed that they were a failure, unworthy of love, and deserving of punishment.

What we have here is a pattern for cursing a child rather than blessing! There is:

> The punishing/abusive touch.
> Harsh/reactionary words.
> A message of disappointment.
> Prediction of an undesirable future.
> Application of distance and shame.

Instead of the biblical theme, "I am blessed to be a blessing," such wounded people live by the demonic creed, "I am a failure and deserving of blame and punishment."

## *The Results of Living with a Fear of Failure*

There are a variety of dysfunctional responses that are manifested by people who fear failure. Each is rooted in emotional woundings that leave people feeling inferior, unable to measure up, likely to fall short in life, unworthy of love, and most of all deserving of punishment. The particular examples below most often occur when a person has made a mistake or fears potential failure in a task or relationship.

## Self-Cursing

First, and probably most common, an individual curses themselves upon making a mistake. They regularly make statements like, "I'm such an idiot! Nothing I do ever turns out right. If it can be messed up, I'll do it! It's no wonder I don't have any friends; I'm so dumb!" These and countless other self-depreciating statements both reveal and reinforce deep inner wounds and feelings of inferiority.

At one time, a member on my staff regularly fed herself with such destructive statements. In a private conversation I politely brought up the subject, wondering if she was aware of this habit. My colleague became tearful and shared how a childhood struggle with dyslexia brought similar comments from teachers and her parents. Even though she was a highly educated woman, her response to failure revealed how she truly felt about herself.

## Self-Punishment

Second, people who struggle with the fear of failure often punish themselves. If they make a mistake, there is an internal emotional mechanism that seems to kick in, demanding payment. When the failure is somewhat mild, the punishment is less severe. Possibly there will be a verbal berating or the intentional withholding of some pleasure. When more severe, some people will actually do physical harm to themselves.

I have had one counselee tell of punching himself or beating his head against a wall. My wife has a friend who, when emotionally overrun with feelings of failure, slices her hands and wrists with razor blades. The intention is not suicide, just cuts deep enough to atone for her mistake. A therapist friend has suggested that such behavior may be an attempt to deal out punishment before God does.

### Evoking Punishment

Third, there are those individuals who evoke punishment from others. For several years I taught an introductory theology course at Simpson College. In one class there was a student who consistently did above-average work. In fact, each assignment was presented on time, insightfully done and far beyond the standard for the actual assignment. It was unquestionable that this student held the highest grade in the class. However, he failed to hand in any work for the final research paper. It was by far the assignment with the most impact on a student's grade. I waited long past the deadline, and still no paper. Ultimately I was forced to give him a very low grade.

It was not until the next semester that I had an opportunity to confront the student about this lapse. Embarrassingly he told me that he had committed an immoral act with a fellow student, and quite frankly did not deserve a good grade. In effect, he was making me the instrument of punishment. He had failed, believed just punishment *must* follow, and so evoked it indirectly from me. Such a dysfunctional way of dealing with sin could only be rooted in past experiences that taught him that failure demands punishment. Deep inside, this young man was wounded and very confused about his worth and identity.

### Self-Justification

There are some people who fear failure to such a degree that they do anything to keep from admitting they have made a mistake. They either build an elaborate system of justifying their behavior or find a likely scapegoat and put all the blame upon him or her.

My children have been involved in organized athletics for years. At one time my son had a coach with an unbelievable inferiority complex. Even his players recognized this. They knew the aberrant behavior he displayed was wrong.

Upon losing a game he always did one of two things. He either blamed a player, the entire team, or terrible officiating. Or he would defend his approach to facing the opponent as the correct one, but then plead his case that they were just a better team. Never once did he admit that his coaching and play selection had any responsibility in the loss. In point of fact, he was a very poor coach and unfortunately remained so because of his unteachable, irresponsible attitude. As parents his behavior bothered us. But as a pastor it was easy to see that deep wounds drove this man. The message of "failure" was constant and loud, and it kept him running and dodging all the time.

### Fear of Being Found Out

A fifth response to the sense of being a failure is relational distance and virtually no vulnerability. Emma attended one of the churches I pastored. She was faithful, attentive, always helpful, and quick to rescue someone in trouble. For some time she attended a small group I was leading and worked very hard at giving everyone the impression that all was well.

Regularly, following prayer and worship, we would go around the group asking, "How are things with your soul?" Emma was always empathetic with anyone in pain. But at the same time she never gave even a glimpse into her own life. Her responses were always the same, "Things are fine; I'm doing well; everything is okay."

One night I received a call from Emma, desperate and wanting to talk immediately. I arranged to meet with her, and she repeatedly said, "I need to share something with you, but promise you won't reject me! Promise!" Her problem was not all that earth-shattering, though important. What became obvious was the fact that Emma feared rejection, feeling unworthy of love. She believed that if anyone ever knew the "real Emma" they would never be her friend. This was but another person in bondage to the lies of the evil one; she was controlled by the lie that she was inferior and deserving of punishment.

## Fear of Taking Risks

Finally, there are those wounded individuals who so fear failure that they are unwilling to take risks. To attempt anything that includes the element of failure is out of the question. Why? Because past failures have made these people feel inferior, unworthy of love, and deserving of punishment. Since their identities are shaped by these lies, to fail again would only remind them that they are in fact failures.

What do the following people have in common? Abraham, Jacob, Isaac, Joseph, Moses, David, Jonah, Peter, and Paul. If you said that each was a Bible hero you would certainly be correct. But they were also men who at times failed miserably! But they were not in themselves failures. Each found his identity in God, not in his performance. Upon failing, they expressed sorrow and repentance, and then confidently moved on to risk again.

It has been said that the only people to never fail are those who never try anything new. The fact is, we all fail! But that does not mean any one of us should view himself or herself as a failure. Only people emotionally wounded by the lies of Satan believe that to fail makes one a failure, unworthy of love, deserving of punishment. If such a person is religious, they often view God as harsh and vindictive, quick to punish, and harm anyone who fails. But be assured of this: such notions are lies of Satan. For every person fighting dysfunctional behavior because of a deep fear of failure, there is good news.

## The Truth Will Set You Free

There is hope and healing for the emotionally wounded, and it is revealed in God's holy Scriptures. I could easily list innumerable Scriptures that describe a new freedom for all who turn to God. It is a transformation of the inner person made possible through the person and work of Jesus Christ. As it relates to the particular dysfunction discussed in this chapter, a passage from Paul's letter to the Romans crystalizes this good news to those who fear failure:

> *But now a righteousness from God, apart from*
> *law, has been made known, to which the Law and*
> *the Prophets testify. This righteousness from God*
> *comes through faith in Jesus Christ to all who*
> *believe. There is no difference, for all have sinned*
> *and fall short of the glory of God, and are justified*
> *freely by his grace through the redemption that*
> *came by Christ Jesus. God presented him as a*
> *sacrifice of atonement, through faith in his blood.*
> *(3:21-25)*

There are several key truths revealed in this passage of Scripture. First, every human being is equal in that all sin, all fail, all fall short of God's requirements (3:23). Failing is the fruit of the fall of Adam and Eve. Separated from God, humans are incapable of living sinlessly, being consistently successful, doing all things perfectly. Such things are impossible for us all!

Second, God, out of great love and grace, has made a way for all us "failures" to be reinstated to our pre-fall status with Him. To be redeemed means to be unique, special, of infinite worth and importance. It means to be viewed as pleasing unto God. It also means we no longer need to fear punishment for our shortcomings.

Third, this is all possible through the work of Jesus Christ! By His death on Calvary He has made full payment for all our sins and failures (3:25). Jesus has fulfilled the requirements of God's law on our behalf. His death becomes the key to our life. His bondage to the cross makes way for our complete freedom— physically, spiritually, and emotionally. Jesus Christ has redeemed us, breaking the chains of Satan's lies that hold us captive and make us dysfunctional!

Fourth, this wonderful healing is available to all who believe (3:22). It is received by faith in Jesus Christ, freely given by the grace of God (3:22, 29). There is no way we could ever earn it and by our behavior ever deserve it. But God, who is infinitely loving, gives this new identity and freedom as a gift. And it is the gift that truly keeps on giving! To those who place their trust in Christ, never again will God relate to them out of wrath. Instead He calls them His own and extends kindness, patience, love, and ongoing forgiveness.

If you are trapped in dysfunctional behavior because of a fear of failure, let the truth of Christ's redeeming love set you free. Go to Him in prayer, laying out the wounds and sins of your past. Then invite the Holy Spirit to heal those haunting memories and set you free of destructive behavior. Allow the Lord Jesus Christ to lay claim to your entire life. He will reinstate your true inheritance and make you whole.

I want to close by reminding you of the message imprinted on that medallion I referred to previously. But allow me to apply it more specifically. To those who feel hopeless, inferior, convinced that they are failures and unable to change, this message is for you. No matter what you have ever done, regardless of all your failures, by faith in Jesus Christ you are loved, accepted, pleasing, complete, and fully forgiven! You and I will fail, but we are not failures! We are sons and daughters of the living God, heirs of the resources of the kingdom that will never end.

## Chapter Seven

# Shame on Who?

*I*n 1989 my family and I moved from metropolitan New York to northern California. We made our transcontinental journey for several reasons, not the least of which were teaching at Simpson College and starting a new local church. While our target area was Redding, we were tired of suburban living and chose a home in the country.

About twelve miles from Redding is a rural area called Palo Cedro. It is a picturesque community with gently rolling hills and a three-directional view of snow-capped mountains. It is there that we purchased a western-style ranch house on several acres of land.

We quickly populated our quiet retreat with the appropriate animals, totally unaware of the care this lifestyle demands. We invited two dogs, a horse, chickens, and a few sheep into our family. It was not long before we learned that the pastoral image one anticipates in such a setting is often far from the reality of the true day-to-day chores of ranch life. Still, our small home in the country has been a great place of healing and growth for our family. This was especially true during the early days of my illness, when solitude and silence were critical ingredients to my recovery.

Most of our land is covered by small, rather scrubby-looking oak trees. They are not nearly as impressive as their eastern cousins, nor do they display fall colors before dropping their leaves. There is, though, a certain attractiveness to them, and the longer we live in the west, the more we appreciate these less-than-mighty oaks.

But there is one very special tree that blesses our family immeasurably. It stands in the middle of our circle drive, catching everyone's attention as they approach our home. It is an apricot tree that has three glorious stages, each beautiful though quite unique. In the spring, white blossoms and light green leaves grace its limbs. Just looking at it infuses me with new life and anticipation.

By early summer, the leaves are a deeper green and yellow apricots bend the limbs under their weight. While previously unimpressed by the apricot, I now find it delicious, especially when picked at just the proper time. Many of our friends have also enjoyed the fruit of our special tree. More than once my wife has sent bags of apricots home with visitors, receiving back pies, jams, and dried fruits as a result. Everyone sends reports that confirm our conviction about the quality of "our" tree.

The third phase for our apricot tree begins in early fall. The fruit is now gone, and almost as if celebrating a job well done, the leaves turn color. No longer green, each leaf becomes canary yellow. For my family, it serves as a reminder of Pennsylvania in the fall. Cheryl and I grew up in that beautiful state and miss the annual autumn pageant of color. Our lone apricot tree blesses our lives yet again, making fall a time of thankful reflection and remembrance.

There is a fourth stage our apricot tree annually experiences, but it's not worth mentioning. You see, it is the winter phase, a time when no one notices or appreciates this normally special tree. In winter, there are no leaves or blossoms or fruit. The tree just stands there completely naked. Every branch is exposed, revealing a rather awkward-looking skeleton. Some limbs are broken, just hanging on by a small strip of bark. Quite frankly, the tree is ugly in winter, and for my first two years in California, I simply ignored it. There is nothing special about an apricot tree in winter, or so I thought.

I was visiting our local nursery one winter day two years ago. In the course of conversation with the owner, I shared my disappointment regarding the useless nakedness the season imposes upon my otherwise beautiful apricot tree. Wow, did I have my eyes opened to reality! He told me that winter was in fact the most important time of the year for a fruit tree. How it is treated when the leaves are down has direct bearing upon the next year's health and fruit. "Winter," my friend said, "is the time to work with your tree." With the leaves gone, old branches can be pulled away and dead limbs cut off. It is a time for pruning back, enabling the tree to bear even more fruit. And, three times through the winter, the tree should be sprayed to kill potential worms or blight, insuring appealing and tasty apricots in the early summer.

"No," my friend commented, "winter isn't a wasted season for your tree. It is a time when the sap runs deep to give it strength. And with the leaves down, you can go in and help the tree have an even better year than the one before." Since then I have had an entirely new appreciation for the ugliness and nakedness that winter brings. If responded to properly, it is the prelude to new life.

## Creation Illustrates Spiritual Truths

God intentionally designed creation to be informative and illustrative of spiritual truths (Romans 1:20). The cycles of my apricot tree parallel certain aspects of the Christian walk. It serves as a metaphor pointing to the repeatable stages of the growth/fruit-bearing process in a disciple's life.

First, believers often find themselves in periods of new growth. Enhanced by the Holy Spirit, life appears where once death resided. A renewed interest in prayer, outreach, Scripture study, service, or holiness is born within the heart. Properly nourished, this blossoms and begins to show signs of new growth. Such times are full of excitement and great expectation.

Secondly, there are those seasons of genuine fruit-fullness. Answers to prayer come regularly, people are led to Christ, the word is written upon the heart, new ministries are launched, and the old ways of sin give way to the fruits of righteousness. True to our Lord's story of the sower and his seed, a harvest is reaped, some ten, fifty or a hundredfold. The source of growth in this season is Jesus Christ, who infuses His life into our being, anointing the labor of our lives with the presence of the Holy Spirit.

Thirdly, there are certainly seasons of celebration for faithful Christians. During this stage, believers rejoice in the work that God has done in and through their lives. While recognizing the harvest was all of grace, Christians take pride in the strength of Jesus. Boasting in Him, they point to healings, a harvest of souls, reconciled brothers and sisters, and increased holiness. Like the brilliant colors of an Eastern fall, there is a radiance during such times that reflects the glory of our Lord and Savior.

And yes, there is for the Christian a season of winter. It is that time (or times) when God works to insure our health and prepare us for new life and greater fruitfulness. By whatever means He chooses, the Father causes us to stand fully exposed before Him. And if my experience is any indicator, we are often naked and vulnerable before at least a few fellow Christians besides. Why? For the same reason that my apricot tree enters the winter season.

"Winter" for the Christian is that time when the Holy Spirit exposes our wounds, broken places, and unfruitful habits. It is far from pleasant, and even less so if we try to hide or resist His work. The Holy Spirit brings us to such seasons in order to heal, repair the broken places, and remove all that is barren and fruitless. As the Spirit "sprays" His oil upon our lives, He kills that which would otherwise eat away and destroy. These difficult days of winter should never be resisted, for it is then that His work goes deep, strengthening and preparing for greater health and well-being.

Jesus told us that there would be times of pruning in our lives. It was part of His upper room discourse, recorded in John 15. He said:

> *I am the true vine, and my Father is the gardener. He cuts off every branch in me that bears no fruit, while every branch that does bear fruit he prunes so that it will be even more fruitful. You are already clean because of the word I have spoken to you. Remain in me, and I will remain in you. No branch can bear fruit by itself; it must remain in the vine. Neither can you bear fruit unless you remain in me.*
>
> *I am the vine; you are the branches. If a man remains in me and I in him, he will bear much fruit; apart from me you can do nothing. (15:1-5)*

Jesus wanted His followers of every generation to understand the essential nature of pruning and pulling away dead branches. It is necessary for good health and fruitfulness to all who abide in Christ.

Though it is not stated in the passage, pruning demands nakedness. Only with the leaves down can the Gardener find the broken and barren places of our lives. In the winter, the branch is absolutely vulnerable. While it is frightening to be so exposed, it is essential to our spiritual and emotional well-being.

Though Jesus taught believers to anticipate "winter nakedness," Christians avoid this stage; we all want to bear fruit for the kingdom, but there is an unquestionable fear of genuine openness and vulnerability. I know—I developed my own coping mechanisms and cosmetics to keep my brokenness out of sight. Yet in my case the Lord allowed the winter winds to blow so fiercely that there I stood, naked and fully exposed.

Too ill to hide, too sick to grab for leaves and glue, I just stood there—broken limbs and barren branches in full view. Unwilling to tolerate my hiding any longer, God put me in a place of absolute dependence. I thank Him for such love—and now I campaign for my brothers and sisters to stop hiding and covering up. "Winter" is a very important part of our spiritual developmental cycle.

## Why Do We Hide Our Brokenness?

There is a powerful emotional component that compels people, even Christians, to resist openness and vulnerability. That component is shame. In *Shame-Free Parenting*, Sandra Wilson defines shame as:

> . . . a soul-deep sense that there is something uniquely wrong with me that is not wrong with you or anyone else in the world. Because I am not perfect and problem-free, I feel hopelessly, disgustingly different and worth less than other people. I view myself as, literally,

worthless. It isn't just that I make a mistake
when I make a mistake; I am a mistake when I
make a mistake. This is shame's message.[1]

Most Christians fear "winter" because it threatens
to expose those ugly scars, open wounds, and fruitless places in their lives. Convinced that he or she
alone has such problems hidden beneath the surface,
he or she anticipates rejection, humiliation, and disqualification. Of course that is a lie born in hell. Like
a concealed cancer, hiding will continue to allow
disease and dysfunction to spread until it ultimately
destroys its victim.

Returning to Genesis, we read in 2:25, "The man and
his wife were both naked, and they felt no shame."
This was the last comment made about Adam and Eve
in their pre-fallen state. They stood totally open,
naked, and vulnerable before God and one another.
They were secure in their self-image, unconcerned
that someone could see into the very depths of their
being. They had worth, were unique and special; far
from a mistake, they were perfect! Not only was there
no need to cover themselves, they delighted in each
other's beautiful nakedness, pure and undefiled.

But notice their response upon eating of the forbid-
den fruit. Immediately they moved from openness to
shame. Realizing what they did, now insecure and
fearing rejection, Adam and Eve sewed fig leaves
together to cover themselves (Genesis 3:6-7). And

---

[1] Sandra D. Wilson, Ph.D., *Shame Free Parenting* (Downer's Grove, IL: Inter-
Varsity, 1992), p. 14.

they quickly went into hiding—from God, from each other, and from themselves. Their sin brought on a many-faceted bondage, not the least of which included feelings of inferiority, worthlessness, and personal disgust. Rather than face up to their sin, Adam and Eve covered up! And for every generation since, people have continued to hide. They hide through approval, performance, religious activity, and countless other pretentious cosmetics. Shame-based hiding is one of the strongest demonic footholds in the family, the church, and society as a whole.

## Shame: The Devil's Stronghold

For three months I preached on inner healing. About midway through the series I commented on the problem and power of shame. It was not the central topic of that particular sermon, merely a point along the way.

I well remember an unusual sense of oppression as I briefly talked to the congregation about shame. The microphone began squealing; there was an unusual number of people getting up to leave; babies began crying; and I had great difficulty focusing. My impression was that it was in fact a demonic attack. Not wanting to jump to conclusions, I gathered elders, staff, and other discerning leaders to discuss their impressions and receive guidance.

I was not surprised to discover that these congregational leaders shared my opinion. In fact, several said they not only felt the spiritual oppression, but were compelled to immediately begin interceding for me. This confirmed my feelings and motivated me to press in further on the subject. I decided to spend one Sunday preaching on the destructive power of shame. For two weeks prior to my presentation our intercessory prayer network diligently prayed. We concluded that shame, that sense of inferiority, unique lack of worth and hopelessness, was a major stronghold of the evil one. It was imperative that we break the enemy's hold through prayer and God's Word. Once broken, it was our hope that people would choose vulnerability, allowing God to work in those hidden areas. His "wind" did blow that day and countless people willingly entered the "winter" season so necessary to healing and fruitfulness.

We have already established several things in our discussion of inner healing. Countless people feel permanently spoiled because of (a) some abuse experienced while children or adolescents, (b) something sinful they had themselves done, whether in adolescence or adulthood, or (c) something they are presently doing that is sinful and destructive.

Satan works hard to bind such individuals with deep feelings of hopelessness and an inability to change. The root of this lie is the stronghold of shame, a state of being that cripples and destroys. Appealing to that sense of permanent unworthiness, the evil one sends a barrage of lies into the victim's mind. "What was done to you or you are doing is so bad you will never be forgiven. You have struggled with this memory or sin for so long that there can be no freedom. What you experienced or are doing is so ugly people will reject you." Based upon these lies, Satan comes bringing his hellish prescription: "Hide!"

The enemy wants people to refuse the "winter" at all cost. "Apply the cosmetics, stay covered, put up the religious facade." This is his scheme! If people believe his lies and follow his dark strategy, the sap never goes deep! Instead perpetual bondage keeps Christians from their blood-bought inheritance. The pain of shame controls every action and influences each relationship. Over time, shame becomes a state of being that eventually leaves the tree of their life desolate. Without the nakedness and vulnerability of the "winter cycle," the broken and battered and barren aspects of our lives remain. Fearing rejection, we hide, not realizing that far from protecting us, it will ultimately destroy.

I have already mentioned God's severe mercy in forcing me out of hiding through depression and agoraphobia. As painful as this "personal wilderness" was, I count it one of life's greatest blessings. The winds of winter left me naked, and thankfully there was no place to hide.

To varying degrees my broken limbs and barren places were open for inspection. In general terms my entire congregation knew about my emotional woundings and dysfunctions. Those closest to me—family, intimate friends, and professional caregivers—knew the specific details. I shared with those closest to me the innermost secrets of my life. God used my vulnerability and their accountability to enhance my recovery.

I have one particular friend, David, whom I felt free to let in with no conditions or restrictions. I have known Dave for more than a decade. He is a bright, intelligent colleague who has as steady and consistent a personality as can be found. Over the years he has been the first person I would seek out for advice, counsel, or encouragement. David is a genuine friend who has shown me unconditional Christlike love.

Probably because I felt so safe with Dave, he was one of the first people outside of my family I turned to for help. As I sensed myself slipping into the darkness, I told Cheryl to "call Dave." All throughout my illness and long season of recovery, Dave was on the inside. He saw me at my worst, heard the ugly stories of my dysfunctional past, and listened as I poured out my heart to God. Dave is a trusted friend. He knows the wounds, sins, and issues that were addressed in my winter, and I feel confident that he respects my emotions and can be thoroughly trusted with the knowledge that is at his disposal.

But one day I found out something about Dave that amazed me. We were riding along talking about the Lord and what He was doing in our lives. Dave told me that the Holy Spirit was beginning to address issues of his past. Particularly, He was peeling back layers of defensiveness to reveal serious emotional woundings in Dave's life.

My friend shared very hesitantly and cautiously. He mentioned no details or specific issues, just the general need for inner healing. In the course of the conversation I asked Dave to share his hurts. I felt concerned and wanted to listen, pray, and possibly be an instrument of healing. Dave's response to my suggestion somewhat shocked me. He said, "I know I need to deal with some specific issues and confess them before someone. But . . . I . . . I can't tell *you*!"

"Why, Dave?" I asked. "I love you and you know I would keep it confidential."

He responded, "It . . . it isn't that. I'm afraid if I tell you what I'm dealing with that you will reject me or be disappointed."

I was almost speechless! We have been friends for years. And Dave knows me like few people on earth—past wounds, ugly sins, dysfunctional behavior and all! He had seen my broken limbs and barren places in full view. What could possibly give him the impression I would reject him? By all rights he should, by human standards, tell me to take a hike. How could he even think that I would violate his trust or fail to honor his wounds? What impression did I leave that would ever suggest I would reject him?

I asked Dave every possible question. Had I hurt him in some way? Was there a specific reason he could not trust me? Did he fear I would tell someone else? Had I somehow given him the idea I was his friend because he was perfect? What was it? To each inquiry Dave responded, "No, it's not that, I'm just afraid you would reject me!"

I thought about this lengthy conversation for days. And finally I realized the root problem. There was a stronghold of shame in David. Somewhere in the past, probably in childhood or adolescence, Dave was wounded by some significant other or others. The message of inferiority, being less than, failing to measure up, or being distortedly different was spoken into his life. Though redeemed by God and given an entirely new and Christlike identity, deep within Dave felt ugly. Satan attacked Dave from the stronghold of shame, though it was nothing more than a fortress of lies. Shame is a powerful force, and in this case worked to keep David in hiding. It held him in chains, even though he watched me go through the same thing, gaining victory only through openness, vulnerability, and the truth of God's Word. Shame is a powerful behavior modifier.

## We Live in a Shame-Based Society

It is common knowledge that television shapes our cultural values and morals. Objectively watch commercials for an evening and anyone can come away with a clear picture of what people value most. For late twentieth-century America, image is everything. Society values beauty, perfection, power, and popularity. Our heroes are men and women who "appear" to have it all. Television has distorted our sense of reality, creating an illusionary world where high-paid athletes, high-profile actors, and high-powered politicians are heroes. It really does not matter if these "models" are shallow, immature, or immoral. Premium is placed on looking right, having the right possessions, belonging to the right group, and being in the right places.

Capitalizing on this distorted view of that which is important, companies market their products with promises that "you, too, can have beauty, perfection, power, and popularity. Just purchase our cosmetics . . . automobile . . . swimwear . . . diet plan . . . tennis shoes . . . undergarments . . . alcoholic beverage . . . or designer jeans." Conversely, if you don't have "the right stuff" you are a geek, nerd, loser, mistake, or dinosaur.

This obsession has gone so far as to send people rushing to weight loss centers, plastic surgeons, and power gurus. Youth, desperate to belong, demand an "in" wardrobe or suffer rejection and isolation. Violent crimes have been committed by teens trying to steal jackets or tennis shoes that are status symbols in their cultural grouping.

The entire campaign is shame-based and quite powerful. The message is clear: fail to measure up and you are a loser, a mistake! The psychological impact on teenagers alone is staggering. Teen suicide is skyrocketing, as are cases of young people with eating disorders, chemical dependencies, and alcoholism.

These problems are symptomatic of great emotional upheaval. Deep within people fear that someone might find out "things are not as they appear." If anyone else saw their "true self," rejection and ridicule would surely follow. A person must work hard to appear right, though deep inside everything is wrong.

One might argue that while society is shame-based, the family unit is potentially strong enough to counter its destructive message. That is certainly true and many families have God's grace securely in place. Some parents have and are teaching their children about the message of forgiveness, righteousness through Christ, and God's acceptance.

But frankly, such families are the rare exception. The norm is that the vast majority of parents are raising their children from the identical shame-based value system as the society in which they live. Standards of perfectionistic performance and appearance are idealized. Wounded parents live in denial regarding their own problems, while simultaneously pushing their children to "look" right, project the proper image, and measure up to expectations. If a child makes a mistake, ridicule and abuse begin in order to modify the behavior. What ultimately results is a deeply wounded child who will grow into a severely dysfunctional adult.

## Wounded in Christian Homes

The wounds of shame are not caused by non-Christian parents alone. Countless adults struggling with wounds incurred in childhood were raised in Christian homes. However, they were in families where legalism replaced grace, performance was more important than inner development, and sin was kept in hiding according to strict rules of secrecy.

Liza Herring is an adult child of an abusive parent. Today, Liza is a respected professional in the medical field. She also lectures on child abuse and molestation. I have known Liza for several years, having met her when she was a teenager in our local youth program. I did not know the truth behind all appearances until years after leaving that church.

The Herring family was thoroughly integrated into the life of their local church. Dad served on the governing council, Mom and daughters sang in the choir, and their youngest son was active in the junior department. They were upbeat, deeply involved, and highly respected in the congregation.

However, as is so often the case in abusive homes, things were not as they appeared to be. Recently Liza called and said, "You didn't know what was really going on in our home, did you?" I was shocked as she shared her tale of parental denial, strict discipline, physically abusive outbursts, and clear rules of silence.

Liza said she and her brother and sisters tried desperately to obey the rules in order to keep the peace. Yet the slightest deviance could be reason enough for ridicule, humiliation, and physical punishment. This environment deeply wounded the entire family, including Liza's mother. Behind the smiles and often humorous behavior of the Herring children were feelings of inferiority, worthlessness, and shame. Only now, as adult children of abuse, are they opening up to the truth. While the vulnerability of the "winter" season is painful for them, it is God's grand and grace-filled prelude to freedom.

The answer to shame-based behavior is found in and through Jesus Christ. But do not assume that pastors and local congregations are above shaming. They are not! While there is a "grace" revolution occurring in many churches today, most congregations are bound by the same practices identified in our shame-based society and shame-based homes. The language is simply changed to fit the church context.

Innumerable churches and entire denominations place performance over genuine spiritual development. Legalistic rules of proper and improper behavior abound. "Real Christians don't dance, swear, drink alcoholic beverages, go to theaters, play cards, wear makeup, or watch television." Rather than teach Christians to walk according to the Spirit, the local church or pastor spells out right and wrong in detail. Along with this is the familiar message that failure or compromise is a clear sign of blatant carnality, leading to rebuke and, if necessary, rejection.

In addition, pastors are often trained to enlist volunteers through guilt, manipulation, and if necessary, shame. Scriptures are used as a whip to keep people moving and in line, rather than the Bread that nourishes, the Water that cleanses, and the Oil that brings healing.

This type of atmosphere is spiritually abusive. It keeps people locked up with their pain, fearing rejection. Members work hard to look good, do more, and keep the rules—all standards of "true spiritually."

In congregations such as these, "winter" never comes. It isn't allowed! After all, "what will people think if they find out how I really feel or what I am secretly doing?" Churches with shame-based ministries drive their people—and even their pastors—into hiding.

I had an opportunity to talk at length to a pastor from a well-known denomination who was in recovery. He very confidentially shared that he had previously struggled with an addiction to pornography. Upon confessing this to his superior he was, by mandate, enrolled into an inpatient treatment program. There he faced his wounds and confronted the multi-faceted issues that led to sexual addiction. This action was very important to his healing.

However, I question other aspects of his superior's intervention. He told this young pastor to keep silent about his problem. The denominational leaders would explain to the pastor's congregation that he was sent on a "special, confidential assignment." This would "preserve his integrity" once he returned from treatment.

Such hiding may pay short-term dividends but in the long run it only leads to dysfunctional behavior. This young man lives with a fear that somehow someone will find out. It also hinders the freedom of people under his care. First, they are not given a model of the kind of honesty and confession that leads to healing. Secondly, he is restricted from having a marvelous and powerful ministry as a wounded healer to the sexually addicted.

All of society, innumerable families, and far too many churches are caught in the wounding cycle of shame. The only remedy is the clear proclamation of the grace-based truth that brings freedom and healing.

Jesus is God's remedy for the broken people dominated by the enemy's lies. To you or anyone you know being eaten away by shame, I rejoice in declaring hope, transformation, and joy that can be yours in Christ. It is there for all who willingly enter the Holy Spirit's winter, a prelude to new life.

## Shame on Me!

Few children have escaped the oft-repeated phrase "shame on you." Many are now adults still struggling to hide the effects of this destructive curse. The pain of shame breeds feelings of hopelessness and low self-esteem. This in turn births destructive coping mechanisms and dysfunctional behavior. The bondage shame brings is almost indescribable, and Satan would have those who are caught in its chains believe the condition is hopeless. But, my friend, that too is a lie.

Once again we come to the healing power of the Lord Jesus Christ. God, while despising sin, does in fact love sinners. He demonstrated the depth and quality of his love by sending His Son Jesus as our Savior and Lord (Romans 5:8). He offers salvation to one and all, not willing that any should perish (2 Peter 3:9).

This salvation, purchased upon Calvary and offered by grace, is unfathomable in its riches. It provides all that a person needs to experience freedom and live a godly life (1:3). That means the person bound by shame can be set free through the redemptive work of Christ. Don't read these words without considering the full impact of their message.

Deep inside you may be plagued by a stronghold of shame. It may be rooted in things done to you in childhood, or some failure on your part. Satan harasses, convincing you that the damage is irreparable. His lies keep you in hiding, fearing rejection and humiliation. But, the Word of God is not "shame on you." Instead, Jesus tenderly says, "Place the shame on Me!" He bore the curse of our failures. This means that Christ is willing to forgive you of all transgressions. And most importantly, it means that you are born again in Christ. By accepting Him, you are made brand new. Paul said it this way: "If anyone is in Christ, he is a new creation; the old has gone, the new has come!" (2 Corinthians 5:17).

This is the truth! And this truth can set you free. As the Holy Spirit brings healing to the hurts of your past, He reveals the truth of your new identity. You are not a mistake! You are not uniquely wrong and distorted! You are not disgusting and different! Through Christ, all this is past, washed away by the blood of the Lamb!

The truth is that because of Jesus you are free, a child of God, precious to the Most High, heir of eternal blessings, a saint who is secure in your grace-given identity. Declare this truth in the face of the evil one! Proclaim this truth as you walk along the path to wholeness! Shout this truth as testimony to the Savior who bore your shame. Sing a new song of joy as the Holy Spirit infuses you with the confidence, peace, perseverance, and presence of the Redeemer. You are a new creation in Christ Jesus!

## Chapter Eight

# Prayer and Inner Healing

*C*heryl and I had been concerned about Rachel Crawford's emotional health for some time. She was relationally dysfunctional, wearing herself out people-pleasing and rescuing. We tried to address the issue with her, only to be politely yet effectively ignored. Rachel's behavior was not only problematic to her own well-being, but it affected her family, friends, and Christian co-workers.

As often happens, Rachel's dysfunctional behavior took a greater and greater toll. Finally, she entered a season of deep depression. Her husband told us that he often came home from work, and found her lying on the couch in the fetal position, crying uncontrollably.

For many of us "bottoming out" is the only way to get us to cry "uncle." Rachel was now willing to follow our advice and receive therapy. We knew, because of my own experience, that healing might involve a variety of approaches and be a long-term process.

However, after months of therapy, including a short, intensive inpatient program, Rachel was not making noticeable progress. She continued her downward spiral into hopelessness. Frustrated, she called to talk. Actually, Rachel was crying out, asking one very important question, "Why am I not getting better?"

Quite frankly I was asking myself the same question. Having been through extensive therapy I quizzed her regarding the treatment she was receiving. "Have they identified specific woundings from your past? Are you receiving cognitive and behavioral instruction? What types of assignments do you receive, and are you doing them? Are you taking your prescribed medications?" Every answer seemed to indicate that basic issues were being addressed.

But then I asked Rachel this question. "Rachel, has your therapist or psychiatrist begun the process of inner healing prayer?" Rachel immediately said, "Prayer? I have been in therapy for months and not one single prayer has ever been uttered! Not by my therapist or psychiatrist—I know they are Christians, but no one has prayed with me about anything!"

I did not need to ask any other questions. Emotional healing cannot happen apart from prayer. Not just a quick opening prayer before a session, but aggressive, multi-faceted, Spirit-filled prayer. While medicine, cognitive and behavior therapy are helpful, prayer is the most essential ingredient on the pathway to inner healing. I link my ongoing well-being to various types of prayer, more than any other aspect of my inner healing. To say the least, I referred Rachel to a therapist who was not only a Christian, but gifted in prayer therapy. After her first session, she called and had new hope and strength to combat the devastating affects of her woundedness.

## *The Priority of Prayer*

John Wesley said, "God will do nothing but in answer to prayer." He did not receive this insight by direct revelation from God. It was the obvious conclusion to his examination of Scripture and the history of the church.

Jesus was a man of prayer. It was His custom to get apart from the crowd and speak with God. Mark writes,

> *Very early in the morning, while it was still dark, Jesus got up, left the house and went off to a solitary place, where he prayed. (Mark 1:35)*

This was not an isolated incident, but a priority in the life of our Lord.

The late David Watson reviewed the various aspects of our Lord's pattern of prayer in his book *Called and Committed*. He pointed to seven particular contexts in which Jesus prayed, modeling a pattern for His followers of every century. Watson noted our Lord in prayer:

1. Every morning.
2. Before making important decisions, such as the calling of the twelve.
3. Whenever He was under pressure, as in the case recorded by Mark 1:35ff.
4. When He was concerned about others, particularly those under attack from Satan.
5. When He Himself was tempted, as evidenced in Gethsemane before his arrest.
6. During His time of pain on Calvary.
7. At the moment of His death, when He committed His spirit unto the Father.

Watson's intent was to provide Christians with insights on prayer from Jesus that could be integrated into their own spiritual development.[1]

Certainly the disciples recognized the priority of prayer in the life of Jesus. Of all they saw Jesus do, the one discipline they wanted to learn was prayer. By watching Jesus they learned that prayer was the key to intimacy with God the Father and empowerment for kingdom ministry. Luke records their request in chapter 11. After seeing Jesus pray, the disciples said, "Lord, teach us to pray" (11:1). Jesus proceeded to give the disciples a model of prayer, known to us as "The Lord's Prayer." He also taught the disciples that persistence in prayer is critical, using a parable as a window of understanding. Finally, in Luke 11:11-13 Jesus assured the disciples that the heavenly Father

---

[1] David Watson, *Called and Committed* (Wheaton, IL: Harold Shaw, 1982), pp. 92-95.

will be faithful to answer prayer.

Jesus, in other contexts, taught additional principles of prayer, some of which are almost staggering in their significance.

> *I will do whatever you ask in my name, so that the Son may bring glory to the Father. You may ask me for anything in my name, and I will do it. (John 14:13-14)*

> *If you remain in me and my words remain in you, ask whatever you wish, and it will be given you. (15:7)*

> *Ask and it will be given to you; seek and you will find; knock and the door will be opened to you. For everyone who asks receives; he who seeks finds; and to him who knocks, the door will be opened. (Luke 11:9-10)*

The disciples caught the Lord's passion for prayer and made it a priority in their own lives. Prayer was the grand prelude to Pentecost, as recorded in the first chapter of Acts. It also was one of the first disciplines taught to new disciples upon their conversion (Acts 2:42). And in the early and difficult days of the Church, prayer opened the door to numerous manifestations of God's power and deliverance (4:28-31; 12:1-19).

As the disciples, particularly Paul, began to instruct the early church, prayer was always identified as necessary for effective Christian living, service, and spiritual warfare. Consider just a few texts where prayer is prioritized in their writings:

- Pray continually (1 Thessalonians 5:16-17).
- Is anyone of you in trouble . . . pray (James 5:13).
- Devote yourselves to prayer (1 Corinthians 7:5).
- Pray for all the saints (Ephesians 5:18).
- Pray in the spirit (5:18).
- Pray on all occasions (5:18).
- Pray for each other (James 5:16).
- Pray . . . that God may open a door (Colossians 4:3).
- The prayer of a righteous man is powerful and effective (James 5:16).

These Scriptures represent but a small portion of what God's Word teaches regarding prayer. The Bible links it to every aspect of individual and corporate well-being. No responsible Christian servant could even suggest the possibility of a fruitful life or effective ministry apart from prayer.

Christians throughout church history caught our Lord's vision for prayer. Name a man or woman of the past twenty centuries who has impacted the world for Christ, and you will find a person devoted to prayer. Brother Lawrence, Theresa of Avila, Martin Luther, John Knox, Jonathan Edwards, George Whitefield, John Wesley, D.L. Moody, A.B. Simpson, Andrew Murray, Charles Spurgeon, E.M. Bounds, Rees Howells, Evelyn Underhill, Billy Graham,

Richard Foster; the list goes on and on. At the heart of every effective servant of the Lord has been the discipline of prayer. It has been the place of intimacy with God and the source of all lasting kingdom service. Possibly E.M. Bounds summed it up best when he wrote, "The effectual, fervent prayer has been the mightiest weapon of God's mightiest soldiers."[2]

To suggest that a person could break the bondage of behavioral dysfunction, recover from depression, fear or obsessive thinking, or be healed of damaged emotions apart from prayer is ludicrous! Given the testimony of Scripture and twenty centuries of church history, to effect deep, lasting change there must be a network of prayer support and prayer therapy. Given its place in my own inner healing, I would question the credibility of any Christian therapist who minimizes or overlooks prayer as a tool for spiritual and emotional healing. As I step back and look at the ingredients that came together to effect my own transformation, prayer stands out as of first importance.

## *The Practice of Prayer*

As you or someone you know begins to move toward wholeness, a regular and balanced time of prayer must be initiated. It is key to renouncing lies, embracing truth, and enlisting divine intervention during the wilderness experience. No matter how bad the situation or how ill one becomes, prayer is an investment in health one cannot afford not to make.

---

[2] E.M. Bounds, *Power Through Prayer* (Grand Rapids, MI: Baker, 1972), p. 42.

Even in my darkest hour and weakest period, prayer helped. What follows is a look into three types of prayer that God used in my healing: the pattern of my own prayer life; the place of intercessory prayer; and the practice of inner healing prayer for the healing of past wounds and painful memories.

Prior to my illness, I had read many books on prayer. I knew it was an important spiritual discipline, but for years practiced it very little. But in 1984 the Holy Spirit impressed on me the absolute necessity of developing an effective and regular prayer life. God used several books to impact my thinking, not the least of which were *The Prayer Life* by Andrew Murray, *Power Through Prayer* by E.M. Bounds, and *Practicing the Presence of God* by Brother Lawrence.

Out of this season of instruction came a new passion and understanding of prayer. I surrendered my "unwillingness" to God, and He replaced it with an appetite to meet with Him regularly. I also recognized that prayer was a discipline, and so adopted a format that fit my personality. The pattern that I found best was an adaptation of the Lord's prayer.

For about eight years I regularly met the Lord in such prayer. Sometimes I would linger for thirty minutes, and at other times upwards of an hour. I carried a journal that contained an outline for prayer, which served to keep my mind from wandering. It proved helpful and very fruitful in my spiritual development, and a means to effect change for people I was praying for as well.

While I appreciated the impact this discipline was having, I had no idea as to its vital importance until I fell ill. Suddenly prayer became necessary to my very existence and health. The foundation God had laid for eight years grew into a fortress for my own sanity, a haven of ongoing healing, and a base of operations to attack the evil one. Though isolated by my doctor for rest and unable to minister, my prayer life expanded immeasurably. Frankly, it was my lifeline. Without prayer I believe I would have gone down!

For several months seasons of prayer were my only moments of peace. I was led to increase my time before the Lord, some days praying three, five, even seven hours. There was nothing noble about this; it was a necessity. I want to share the basic pattern I used in prayer, believing it can serve others in the time of storm and darkness. I remind you that what follows is an approach to prayer built upon the Lord's Prayer. Also, as I will mention, it contains key ingredients for the person seeking inner healing.

First, begin your time of prayer by focusing upon the Lord Jesus Christ. It is His work on Calvary that gives a person their new identity and standing before God. By His blood, believers are transformed into sons and daughters of God. Christians are welcomed into God's presence, able to call him "Daddy," confident of his acceptance and concern. In Hebrews 10:19-22 we read:

> *Therefore, brothers, since we have confidence to enter the Most Holy Place by the blood of Jesus, by a new and living way opened for us through the curtain, that is, his body, and since we have a great priest over the house of God, let us draw near to God with a sincere heart in full assurance of faith.*

Anyone dwelling upon these truths is already effecting their own inner healing, dispelling the lies of Satan that seek to destroy. Through the cross we can come to God in great confidence regardless of past failures and wounds!

Next, begin to praise and hallow God the Father for who He is, what He is like, and the things He does. Within my prayer outline I have written the following:

*Names of God*
Yahweh-jireh—The Lord Provider
Yahweh-M'Kaddesh—The Lord who Sanctifies
Yahweh-rophe—The Lord who Heals
Yahweh-shalom—The Lord is my Peace
Yahweh-rohi—The Lord is my Shepherd
Yahweh-nissi—The Lord is my Banner
Yahweh-shammah—The Lord is There

*Nature and Attributes of God*

| | |
|---|---|
| Holy | Sovereign |
| Loving | Infinite |
| Benevolent | Eternal |
| Gracious | Righteous |
| Merciful | Just |
| Patient | Omnipresent |
| Faithful | Omnipotent |
| Omniscient | Compassionate |
| True | |

*The Work of God*

| | |
|---|---|
| My Redeemer | My Loving Father |
| My Deliverer | My Resting Place |

| My Refuge | My Shelter in Time of Storm |
| My Shield | My Light upon the Path |
| My Hiding Place | My Rock to Stand Upon |
| My Stronghold | My Strong Tower |
| My Creator | My Mighty Warrior |

Consider any one or more of these truths, ascribing glory to God with words, songs, and shouts of praise. Dwelling on God and His majesty infuses the believer with life and hope in the darkest hour. To praise Him also pushes back the evil one, while instilling the principles of truth deeper and deeper in the believer's heart (Isaiah 30:32; Psalm 8:2; Psalm 149:6-9). Remember the strongholds of fear, rejection, failure, performance, and shame are based upon lies. Many of us have believed and acted upon these lies for years. Therefore, the infusion of truth is critical to tearing down strongholds, taking thoughts captive, and receiving the healing God provides in Christ Jesus.

Third, it is important to pray that God establish His kingdom work and will. In other words, the believer must say yes to what God is doing and wants to do in his or her life. That includes the act of surrender to His sovereign work, even during the wilderness experience. While I in no way enjoyed what I was experiencing, I knew God was in it. And as difficult as it was, surrendering to His work, in His way, in His time was key to my healing.

On August 8, 1992, just three months into my illness, I stopped to record in my journal. I was still in depression, agoraphobic, and full of obsessive-compulsive thoughts. But I knew God was at work, so I wrote down specific changes that had already occurred through this "wilderness." I recorded all the good things coming out of the trial and listed areas that God identified as needing serious attention. There are twenty-three issues listed! All important and each life-changing! I wrote that long before I entered therapy and went through inner healing. If I were to add to the list now, it would number nearly a hundred such changes. God does use bad things for good purposes if we surrender to His will!

Next there is the issue of our daily needs. Jesus and Paul both taught believers to live life one day at a time. They also emphasized the importance of trusting God for all you need for the moment by seeking first the kingdom. Traditionally, "our daily bread" is a time to pray for food, finances, and other material needs. For the person going through inner healing, it takes on a whole new meaning.

For years I lived for tomorrow. I was driven and very goal-oriented. I not only had enough energy for today, but enough to dream and work for many tomorrows to come. That all changed when depression set in upon me. Suddenly I found myself needing to pray moment by moment, let alone one day at a time. Countless times I prayed, "Lord, if You don't hold on to me in this moment, I believe I will lose my mind." Within one or two minutes I needed to pray the same prayer yet again!

I did not know if I even had a future. How would bills be paid if I lost my job? What if I needed to be institutionalized? Where would Cheryl and the children live if something happened to me? Could I hold on for just one more day? Now, it was all up to God. He became my moment by moment, day by day Source. And to those who are suffering, fearful, and trying to hold on, I offer encouragement. God always came through—moment by moment and day by day. He can be trusted, if we will just rest in Him.

Fifth, the believer must face the matter of forgiveness in prayer. We have discussed this at length already. Regular prayer is often the context where God points out our sin and our unforgiving hearts. And, as detailed in chapter three, forgiveness is essential to inner healing.

More often than not God met me in prayer as I dealt with my sin. He faithfully revealed where I was consistently falling short. The conviction of the Holy Spirit would woo me to repentance, breaking the enemy's grip on various areas of my life. The Lord would also show me situations where I needed to extend forgiveness to others. Sometimes the issues were recent, more often in the distant past. Regardless, I knew the matters were to one degree or another related to my healing and future well-being. To pray, "Forgive us our debts as we forgive our debtors" is therapy at its best!

Next, the believer prays at length regarding protection from the assaults of the evil one and his demonic forces. I want to limit my discussion specifically to the relationship of demonic attack and inner healing. I believe every believer should learn to pray against the forces of the dark one. Here, I want to encourage and equip those who are struggling with past wounds, painful memories, dysfunctional behavior, and emotional upheaval.

For most people the root cause of deep emotional pain is either something done to them, they did themselves, or they are doing. To cope, any one of numerous behaviors and destructive habits are embraced. While they may provide short-term help, in the long run they will ruin a life. Such behaviors are like rotting garbage, repulsive and unhealthy. And know this: garbage attracts rats. Or, in more biblical terms, unconfessed wounds and destructive behavior can be ground for demonic attack.

I will not be discussing the often-asked question, "Can Christians be demon possessed?" Rather, I refer you to *Demon Possession and the Christian* by Fred Dickason, *The Bondage Breaker* by Neil Anderson, and *Spiritual Warfare*, a tape series and workbook by Ed Murphy. These are balanced works on the subject. What I do believe is that Christians can be demonized (a more accurate translation of the Greek word regularly translated "demon possessed"). To be demonized is to be either oppressed, harassed, or affected by a demonic spirit. It feeds upon one's area of weakness, whether that be an emotional wounding, painful memory, past or present sin.

It is critical that the person seeking inner healing have at least a basic understanding of this spiritual battle. Paul said that our true struggle is not against flesh and blood, but rather against the powers of darkness (Ephesians 6:12). He is referring to various levels of demonic attack. Such forces are far too powerful to be fought by mere human power. It takes the strength and power of the Lord that is ours in

Jesus Christ (2:6 and 6:10).

In Ephesians 6 Paul gives specific advice regarding spiritual warfare. Believers should follow his guidance, making it a matter of daily prayer. He gives a threefold strategy to fighting the evil one. First we are instructed to put on the full armor of God. Every day we ought to "pray on" each piece of the armor, for it both protects and empowers Christians to stand firm in the dark hour. In the name of Jesus, pray on:

> *The Belt of Truth*—a declaration that God's Word alone is truth; all else is based on the lies of the enemy.
> *The Breastplate of Righteousness*—a declaration of our new identity and standing before God through Christ.
> *The Shoes of the Gospel of Peace*—a readiness to embrace and communicate reconciliation through the blood of Christ.
> *The Shield of Faith*—a declaration of trust in God regardless of circumstances.
> *The Helmet of Salvation*—the symbol of victory and hope that fills our minds instead of the enemy's lies.
> *The Sword of the Spirit*—God's living word that specifically addresses the harassment and deception of Satan.

Praying on God's armor is a critical exercise of faith with direct impact upon inner healing. It is an armor of truth. Every time a believer prays it on, he or she weakens the enemy's grasp. This prepares the way for freedom and inner healing.

Paul encourages believers to do two additional things to combat the evil one. First, pray on all occasions in the Spirit with all kinds of prayers (6:18). Secondly, be watchful and alert (6:19). Satan is crafty, working hard to deceive believers. We must learn to recognize his destructive strategies, particularly where we are most susceptible to falling. He knows when and how to hit believers, hoping to ensnare and destroy. Prayerfully seek discernment in order to sabotage his efforts by the Word of God. The truth sets us free and keeps us free.

Finally, my prayer time includes interceding for various people. No matter how dark the night, the Christian must pray for others. It is critical to their own inner healing as well as a ministry. I suggest dividing one's intercessory prayer list into three categories. First, those you feel called to pray for permanently. For me, this list is restricted to my immediate family and a few others. Secondly, I suggest a daily list. These are people and concerns you pray for as long as the need exists or burden tarries. Third, make a weekly list, possibly divided into seven parts, one for each day. These concerns are less immediate, but important enough to give some careful attention in prayer.

This represents the pattern of prayer that effected my own inner healing. It took time daily and continues week by week throughout the year. Many times I felt God's intimate presence and the healing effect of this discipline. At other times, it was a difficult battle. But again, personal prayer is one of the most critical elements of emotional healing and well-being. It dare not be overlooked!

## Intercessory Prayer

As important as personal prayer was to my healing, it was not enough. The Holy Spirit quickened an army of intercessors who regularly went before the Lord on my behalf. I received hundreds of letters from people saying, "God has called me to pray for you during your illness." Countless people phoned my wife with the same message. From across the country and around the globe prayers were presented at the throne room of God on my behalf. Unquestionably, intercession is a ministry the Lord uses to effect healing.

The importance of intercessory prayer is emphasized throughout Scripture. Two passages have particularly encouraged me to both intercede and enlist personal intercession. First, in Colossians 4 Paul writes:

> *Epaphras, who is one of you and a servant of Christ Jesus, sends greetings. He is always wrestling in prayer for you, that you may stand firm in all the will of God, mature and fully assured. (4:12)*

Here is a graphic illustration of intercession. A person wrestles in prayer, combating the enemy on behalf of another, praying for God's will and ultimate victory. It is a God-given ministry, motivated by love, empowered by the Spirit, and accomplished in the name of Jesus Christ.

I could share any one of hundreds of letters from people called by God to intercede for me. At any moment of the day and for different lengths of time, one of the Lord's own would share my burden. They were fighting for my freedom and healing, and their ministry was essential.

One of the first breakthroughs during my depression came as I read a letter from a fifteen-year-old girl in our congregation. I want to share part of what she wrote, illustrating how she "wrestled" on my behalf.

Dear Terry,

Wednesday night I was praying for you and God laid this verse upon my heart. "Call unto me and I will answer thee and show thee great and mighty things which thou knowest not" (Jeremiah 33:3, KJV).

Thursday night I was also praying for you and God told me, "Resist the devil and he will flee." I was kind of confused, because I've never had God speak to me before. But God told me, "Captain, put on your armor, this means war." I thought of Ephesians 6 and got up and read it. He then led me to Isaiah 41:10, "Fear not, for I am with thee. Be not dismayed; for I am thy God. I will strengthen thee; yea, I will uphold thee with the right hand of my righteousness" (KJV).

I just want you to know . . . you are not alone in this battle.

Love,

Erica Hemping

As I read this letter something deep happened. For the first time I was crying tears of joy. I knew the Lord was at work and had raised up warriors on my behalf. My friend Erica was certainly one of His captains!

Another story of intercession is recorded in Exodus 17. The Israelites were in battle with the Amalekites at Rephidim. Moses stood on the top of a hill, arms outstretched in intercession, while Joshua fought in the valley. As long as Moses held up his hand, the Israelites were winning. But after time he grew tired and his arms fell to his side. When this occurred the Amalekites began to rout the Israelites.

Upon seeing this Aaron and Hur ran to the top of the hill, each at one side of Moses. Sitting Moses upon a stone, these two men held up his weary arms so that they remained steady until sunset. The account closes with the words, "So Joshua overcame the Amalekite army with the sword" (Exodus 17:13).

Joshua may have overcome the Amalekites with the sword, but not without the intercession of Moses, Aaron and Hur.

Countless men, women, and children contributed to God's victory in my life—intercessors who faithfully petitioned the Lord and pushed back the evil one. Some of these people I know; others will be revealed in glory. Regardless, the battle was not won on my own!

People suffering from emotional woundings and the destructive behavior of dysfunction need to seek God for intercessors. Satan will try to keep the battle in hiding, shaming people into silence. But God's prescription is to confess your needs to one another to enlist prayer support (James 5:16).

I would encourage anyone who is seeking inner healing to read two books: *Possessing the Gates of the Enemy* by Cindy Jacobs, and *The Prayer Shield* by C. Peter Wagner. These books will model, motivate, and instruct on the topic of intercessory prayer. At the very least, they should help the hurting person pray for prayer support.

During the season of inner healing a mighty battle rages. Who will stand before God on your behalf, or that of some other person seeking freedom from destructive behavior? There are no Lone Rangers in this fight! Pray that God will enlist an army of support as you or someone you love walks through the valley of decision! From my perspective, this is not a suggestion, it is a necessity!

## Inner Healing Prayer Therapy

Of all the tools of Christian therapy, none are as vital as time spent with the therapist praying for inner healing. Dr. David Seamands, pastor, author, and counselor, believes it to be vital to the healing of painful memories. Under the guidance of the Holy Spirit, the therapist uses prayer to bring to the surface specific wounds, unleash pent-up emotions, unchain the individual from demonic influence, receive the healing touch of Jesus, and infuse biblical truth where lies once harassed. Such prayer is rooted in the faith that Jesus can and does heal the wounds that reside deep within.

Of such therapeutic prayer Seamands writes:

> This prayer time is the very heart of the
> healing of memories. It is in prayer that the
> healing miracle begins; without it, the whole
> process may simply be a form of auto sugges-
> tion, catharsis, or feeling therapy. This special
> time of prayer cannot be bypassed if there are
> to be lasting results.[3]

Prayer therapy was used of God to set me free from
deep emotional wounds. I can't imagine moving on
to wholeness without this Spirit-directed process. But
I must tell you it was not a therapist that led me
through the sessions. While my steps to recovery
included numerous professional therapists, counselors, and a psychiatrist, none felt comfortable or
well-trained in this method of therapy.

Those who walked me through the process were
laypeople—my wife, a professor friend from Fuller
Theological Seminary, and two laymen from the
church served at various times as God's instruments.
I initiated and at points even instructed in my own
sessions after reading several books outlining the
essentials of prayer therapy. Of particular help were
Seamands' two books, *Healing for Damaged Emotions*
and *Healing of Memories*, and *The Way Out of the Wilderness* by Earl Henslin. One of the laymen found insights from the writings of Neil Anderson equally
helpful.

It may appear to have been a piecemeal process, yet

---

[3] David A. Seamands, *Healing of Memories* (Wheaton, IL: Victor, 1985), p. 27.

God sovereignly led as I "walked back" in time to deep woundings during numerous prayer sessions. Event by event, the Lord pinpointed painful past experiences, unleashed stifled emotions, and brought freedom and healing where pain and anger once reigned. The prayer sessions were Spirit-directed and powerful—and brought a lasting wholeness. Memories that once ignited rage, shame, or depression are now anointed with the Spirit's healing. Forgiveness, understanding, and joy are the fruits of the Lord's deep work—a work that I believe could have only been accomplished by prayer.

Through my own experience, extensive reading, and the Lord's direction, I now use prayer therapy with men and women suffering emotional upheaval and behavioral dysfunction from past hurts. Cheryl and I have seen dramatic results. Certainly it is not the only therapeutic tool, but it is one of the most essential for the emotionally damaged. Using prayer therapy demands preparation and much longer counseling sessions. Normally we schedule two hours and fifteen minutes, staying longer if the Lord so leads.

I believe the best way to describe inner healing prayer is by using a typical session as a model. In this case, the counselee was a young mother filled with rage and dominated by a performance orientation that was ruining her life. She came to us for help that eventually involved approximately fifteen two-and-a-quarter-hour sessions.

Remember, inner healing prayer was only one tool we used. Weekly assignments aimed at cognitive input and behavioral change were regular aspects of our time together. Some sessions we simply listened as our counselee poured out her heart. But there were these very important times when inner healing prayer was God's instrument of healing.

To begin with Cheryl and I find it important to: (a) be in harmony in our relationship, (b) place a high priority on our own times of silence and solitude with the Lord, and (c) pray together about the counselee, regularly seeking the Lord for insight and discernment.

At the initial session we felt led to assign our counselee the task of writing a letter to her father. This letter was not meant to be sent; it was a tool for her therapy. It seemed to us that the core of her dysfunctional behavior was linked to his abusive manner during her childhood and adolescence. We asked her to prayerfully write this letter, detailing what was genuinely on her heart. She was to include specific events that were particularly painful. Before leaving, Cheryl and I prayed for the Holy Spirit's help and protection while doing the assignment. We also encouraged her to write only when she felt led, and as much as possible refrain from over-analysis and worry when not writing.

The next week the three of us began the session with a season of praise. I then invited the Holy Spirit to be the sovereign Counselor throughout our time together. Cheryl and I also prayed on God's armor for protection and as a declaration that truth would be the foundation of all that was about to happen. Finally, we asked Jesus Christ to silence any spirits that would seek to harass or derail the process.

At this point we asked the Holy Spirit to bring to the surface the particular event He wanted to work on for that day. The counselee was advised to trust in the Spirit's involvement, and begin to share the details of the experience He brought to mind. Our style was conversational, moving in and out of prayer as appropriate. Before she began to recount the specific experience, Cheryl and I asked that the Lord bring back to her memory everything necessary for healing.

The counselee then began to tell us and the Lord of a very painful memory. In brief it involved her father raging over what he perceived to be a violation of a clear family rule. He stormed at this young girl in a public setting, spanked her abusively, and then made numerous shaming statements. The ugly irony was that his perception was erroneous. She had not violated the rule, but her pleas to explain went unheeded.

After the counselee detailed this abusive event, we asked the Holy Spirit to unleash the pent-up emotion related to this wounding. We instructed the counselee to imagine that her father was there, and to tell him how she felt and the impact this experience has had upon her. Immediately anger and rage began to pour out. She spoke of the unfairness of the punishment and the frustration at not being heard. She then expressed how this abuse and shaming made her feel. Words like humiliated, violated, worthless, rejected, and insecure were each mentioned. She also verbalized feelings of isolation as her father emotionally distanced himself from her as part of her ongoing punishment. It was meant to be a shaming period aimed at behavior modification.

Throughout this unleashing Cheryl and I prayed, and assured the counselee that it was safe. We expressed the compassion and love of God toward her, much as the Father did to Jesus at Gethsemane.

Once the pain and emotion were fully expressed our prayers shifted. We asked the Lord Jesus to enter that memory with the counselee. Cheryl and I encouraged her to surrender her imagination and "mental vision" to the Lord as instruments of healing. Dr. Seamands refers to this as "sanctified imagination." As the Spirit led, one of the three of us would speak the truth of God's Word into the situation. The counselee imagined Jesus comforting her as she wept following her abuse. Cheryl and I spoke specific Scriptures and truths of Christ's love, acceptance, and compassion. We particularly focused upon her new identity in Christ, worth, uniqueness, and belonging. I asked the Holy Spirit to touch her wounds and bring assurance of her healing and right standing before God. Obviously, this is a brief overview of what was a very lengthy process.

Continuing in the atmosphere of prayer, we moved at the Spirit's leading to two important actions. First, we encouraged the counselee to see her father through the eyes of Jesus and then express forgiveness. This took time and a significant period of waiting. But, faithfully, the Spirit gently led and empowered her to say, "Daddy, I forgive you." Secondly, we led the counselee in prayer, renouncing any foothold Satan had in her life through this event. It now belonged to Jesus Christ and the evil one was not free to use it ever again!

Before closing our time of prayer, we thanked the Lord for His deep work, and sealed all that happened by the power of the Holy Spirit. It was obvious that God had done a great work. Though drained, a new countenance was evident on this young mother's face.

We continued this process event by event over several sessions. The counselee gave testimony in church to a permanent freedom and healing she had not experienced in the past. To God be the glory!

*Chapter Nine*

# The Unsearchable Riches of Christ

One day as I was reflecting upon my own journey toward inner wholeness, two facts stood out boldly in my thinking. First, there were numerous instruments of healing that contributed to my recovery. Some of these were people, like my doctor, psychiatrist, psychologist, therapists, nurses, counselors, friends, and of course my immediate family. Other tools were such things as behavioral training, cognitive input, psychodrama, experiential therapy, books, tapes, and inner healing prayer. To varying degrees each one of these people and processes helped restore my emotional well-being.

But secondly, and far more importantly, I recognized that there was only one source of healing. And that was the person and work of Jesus Christ! He and He alone accomplished that which was necessary for my healing. As grateful as I am to all the instruments of His grace, Jesus is the Great Physician and as such, all glory and honor go to Him!

Behind my dysfunctional behavior were deep feelings of insecurity, inferiority, and rejection. Though I tried to hide behind a facade of performance and workaholism, my emotional wounds eventually worked their way to the surface of my personality. High anxiety led to depression, depression to fear, and fear ultimately to obsessive-compulsive thinking. This all pointed to deep emotional wounds and eventual psychological breakdown.

What prescription or therapeutic process could ever really address such deep needs? Can a pill erase the memory of abuse? Can therapy alone release a person from feelings of inferiority, insecurity, or rejection? Could a book or tape series actually set a person free from fear? Are counselors able, on their own, to disarm that sense of impending doom or death? Do twelve-step programs unleash the chains that bind the chemical abuser, the alcoholic, the child-molester?

Only Jesus Christ has the power to set the captives free! In and of themselves, prescriptions, programs, and processes offer at best short-term relief. But when Christ Jesus is recognized as the source of healing and all else the means of grace, there is great hope for permanent wholeness. Why? Because of Calvary! On the cross Jesus paid the debt, defeated the foe, and insured an inheritance to all who believe.

The root of every abuse, emotional wound, dysfunctional behavior, and addiction was pulled out and destroyed at Golgotha. Practically this means that failure has been forgiven, the rejected have been reconciled to God the Father, the insecure have been placed upon the solid Rock, the broken have been made whole, and the unacceptable received into God's eternal family. Jesus Christ is God's prescription for the fallen human race. And every man, woman and child who receives the Lord by faith is a recipient of His great salvation.

The Apostle Paul, in Second Corinthians, wrote:

> *Now the Lord is the Spirit, and where the Spirit of the Lord is, there is freedom. And we, who with unveiled faces all reflect the Lord's glory, are being transformed into his likeness with ever-increasing glory, which comes from the Lord, who is the Spirit. (3:17-18)*

These two verses are filled with promise for the emotionally wounded. First, Paul assures us that wherever the Spirit of the Lord dwells there is freedom. We know from elsewhere in Scripture that every believer is indwelt by the Holy Spirit (Romans 8:16). This means that we have in fact been free since the moment we accepted Christ. You may ask, "If that is so, why have I lived in bondage even after coming to the Lord?" Because, like I did, you have chosen to believe the lies of Satan rather than walk in the fullness of Christ.

That is why Paul goes on to say that though we are free, we "are being transformed into his likeness with ever-increasing glory, which comes from the Lord, who is the Spirit." In other words, at the moment a person receives Christ he or she obtains all they need for life and godliness. However, most often the new believer is not aware of the fullness of that salvation. A person can continue to live in chains of shame, inferiority, insecurity, or any one of several other bondages. Satan can keep a person in darkness, believing lies that produce dysfunctional and destructive behaviors.

Thus the role of the psychiatrist, therapist, counselor, and every other instrument of grace is to be used of God to turn on the light of truth in the person's inner being. They, under the Holy Spirit's anointing, apply the complete work of Christ to deep emotional wounds. Using a variety of processes, the "instrument" is used by God to identify the wound, bring it into the light of Christ's love, release the bondage of the evil one, and apply the healing power of the Lord. What results is transformation and freedom—a freedom rooted solely in the work of the Lord Jesus!

## Understand Your New Identity

Today as I was working on this chapter, I received a call from a man named Don. He asked to meet with me, saying that he heard I had gone through something similar to what he was presently experiencing. I agreed and set up an appointment for a week from today. Before he even begins to share his story, I already know what he needs.

Don must come to understand his new identity in Christ Jesus! Sure, we will talk about past wounds, destructive behavior, and steps to freedom. But all these are but the various means of grace. Ultimately, healing comes from the Lord of Calvary. He and He alone restores men and women to their pre-fallen position and identity before God. Jesus is the answer!

Paul was given a powerful ministry from God. And, in several epistles he said that at times things were tough. He faced severe opposition and persecution, confessed feelings of fear and weakness, and more than once mentioned facing pressures that seemed more than he could bear. In Second Corinthians 1:8-9, he said, "In our hearts we despaired even of life" (author's paraphrase).

Yet the Apostle Paul said that he did not lose heart (4:1, 16). This statement grabbed my attention when I was suffering from depression. I had lost heart and at times even lost hope. What was Paul's secret? Certainly he faced far more opposition and pressure than I. How was he able to carry on in the face of trouble and not lose heart?

In reading Second Corinthians 4, I found his secret. In truth, the Holy Spirit revealed it to my aching and dismaying heart. First, Paul said he renounced all secret and shameful ways (4:2). In other words, He brought out into the light of Christ any past wounding, sin, or present disobedience. Secondly, he stated that he never distorted God's word. Instead Paul set forth the truth plainly to every person (4:2). And that truth is God's word about the person and work of Jesus Christ. In verses 4-6, Paul says that Jesus is the "light of the gospel," able to "shine out of darkness," causing "light [to] shine in our hearts," giving to believers "the knowledge of the glory of God."

While verses 7-13 go on to speak of difficult times,

Paul continues to point to Jesus as the key to freedom
and life. He assures his readers that this life is not only
for today, but will sustain all believers into and
throughout eternity. He states, "We know that the one
who raised the Lord Jesus from the dead will also
raise us with Jesus and present us with you in his
presence" (4:14). Thus, in spite of all past sins and
present pressures, Jesus was for Paul the key to
wholeness and well-being. And so He is to all who
would believe. And in believing, people must learn
the truth of His unsearchable riches, which can set
them free and transform them into the likeness of
Jesus Christ. This, my friend, is the bare essence of
inner healing.

## In the Face of Christ

Richard Herndon is a deeply wounded young man.
I met him during a course I was teaching on spiritual
formation. At first glance, there was no reason to
suspect that he was in deep emotional pain. In fact, I
was rather impressed by him. Richard is in excellent
physical condition, always polite, well groomed,
prompt, and conscientious with his studies. I noticed
that he was faithful at chapel and church services, and
participated in the college mission program. Yet just
below the surface is an emotional storm of violent
proportions. Richard is angry, confused, bitter, and
consumed with the fear of failure.

Several weeks into the course Richard made an
appointment to see me. It was then I learned that
"things are not as they appear to be." After the cus-
tomary opening remarks, I pressed Richard as to the

nature of his visit. In a stoic, unusually controlled manner he slowly began to speak about the war within him. As is often the case there were a variety of issues, but particularly an intense anger and distrust of God.

Richard had taken theology courses, so he had a cognitive understanding of the nature and attributes of God. But he confessed that though Scripture and theological textbooks may say otherwise, he saw God as demanding, uncaring, and dictatorial. Richard went on to tell me that he *had* to be a missionary. He did not want to serve God on a foreign field, but feared great punishment from God if he refused or delayed. While choosing to go, he was angry and quite bitter.

Time demanded that we schedule another appointment to talk. In praying about his next visit, I felt compelled to ask Richard about his home life. We began our next session with prayer, followed by the predictable "how are things going" questions. But as soon as opportunity afforded itself, I asked Richard to talk about his family. He spoke tenderly of his mother and admiringly about his brothers. But when I asked about his dad, intensity and rigidity were instantly noticeable.

Richard worked with all his might to control his emotions while detailing life with his father. He described a highly legalistic man, strict, emotionally detached, and demanding. Richard said that rules were clearly defined and punishment swift and harsh. His father did not condone outward expressions of emotions, particularly those he considered weak. Yet, his father was given to irrational outbursts at times that made Richard feel very insecure whenever around him.

I caught a glimpse of Richard's rage when he told me, with great hesitation, of a particular family tragedy. His anger was directed at his dad for not allowing him to mourn the death of a close friend. His father said mourning was not appropriate since his friend was now with Jesus. Likewise, he was outraged at God for allowing the fatal accident to occur in the first place. I say I caught a glimpse of Richard's rage because he worked with all his might to stifle the emotions attached to this event. I encouraged him to let go, but he stoically refused. He was afraid that to express his true feelings would most certainly invite the wrath and punishment of God.

It is very difficult to work with someone like Richard. His distorted concept of God, which has obviously been shaped by his father, places him in a powerful trap. His only hope for wholeness is linked to God. Yet nineteen years in his father's household had served to create a caricature of God as hard, unbending, distant, void of compassion, demanding, and quick to punish. Certainly this is *not* the true nature of God, but because God is described in Scripture as our Father, Richard quickly transfers what he experienced with his earthly father to God.

To do this is a terrible mistake, yet innumerable people shape their concept of God in the image of authority figures in their lives. Thus, to the emotionally abandoned or abused, God is distant and uninvolved. To the child reared by a strict disciplinarian,

He is angry and vindictive. If a parent was given to outbursts of rage, God is unpredictable and given to wrath. Parents who demand performance and perfection often raise children who desperately seek to please God and gain His approval. These are but a few examples of the destructive misconceptions of God. To be sure, they are empowered by the evil one, hoping to keep the broken and abused far from any encounter with the genuine God of glory.

How then does freedom come when, like Richard, a person (possibly you) fears drawing near to the One who offers the freedom they so desperately need? In most cases, it does very little good to rehearse Scripture and systematic theology. Why? Because information alone, no matter how true, cannot break the strongholds of distortion. Even Richard said, "I know what the Bible teaches about God, but I still don't trust Him." Past experiences with his primary authority figure left deep wounds, resulting in highly dysfunctional behavior, and deeply ingrained "feelings" about God.

Since Richard could not approach God directly, by what means would he find healing and deliverance? Interestingly, for him and others like him, there was not nearly the distorted emotional baggage attached to his experience of Jesus. He saw Him as gentle and compassionate, the servant Savior and Lord of the Redeemed. Richard said he could pray to Jesus and felt accepted by Him. It was God who was the problem!

Obviously Richard's theology was distorted, since the Father, Son, and Holy Spirit are One. They share the same nature and attributes, one in essence though three in persons. Thus whatever Jesus is like, God is the same! The attributes of the Holy Spirit are likewise the attributes of God the Father. It was most important to Richard's healing that his caricature of God be replaced with knowledge of the true God. And the pathway to this healing was by way of the unsearchable riches of Christ.

## *Jesus, the Radiance of God's Glory*

The Apostle Paul wrote that the way to gain true knowledge of God was by looking into the face of Christ (2 Corinthians 4:6). Elsewhere Scripture says that, "The Son is the radiance of God's glory and the exact representation of his being" (Hebrews 1:3). In other words, if you want to know what God is like, look at Jesus. Read the Gospels and see how He responds to the broken and lost. Look long and hard at the stories of healings, miracles, signs, and wonders. Ponder His teachings on the kingdom and the pathway of servanthood. View His sacrificial death and glorious resurrection. Look full in His wonderful face. Why? Because in Christ God is saying, "This is what I am truly like. This is how I feel about you. This is what I want to do in your life."

We cannot actually look into the face of Christ. However, Scripture describes Him in detail providing a word portrait of the Lord. And what we see in Jesus is the exact representation of God! Was Jesus unapproachable? Hardly. He was surrounded by people. Was He vindictive and angry? Not at all. Jesus was compassionate even to the worst of sinners. Did Jesus come to condemn and destroy? He said that He came not to condemn, but to bring life!

Was Jesus harsh and punitive to those who failed and fell short? No, He offered forgiveness and a new way of life. Did He demand perfect performance before He would accept people? Just look at the disciples and you will see how He extended acceptance to tax collectors, rebels, the uneducated, and undesirable. Now remember this: *Jesus is the exact representation of God!* Look into His face, and you will see God. And God is extending His arms to bring reconciliation and wholeness to all who will turn to Him. We see this in Jesus, and what is true of Jesus is true of God!

John the Apostle looked into the face of Jesus. He saw Jesus in life, death, resurrection, and complete glorification. John heard Him teach, saw Him heal, watched Him with people, and listened as He forgave those who crucified Him. He also was a witness to the resurrection, having seen Jesus alive again after Calvary. Knowing Jesus as He did, what did Jesus teach John about God? Being so intimate with the incarnate Christ, what did John now know about God with more certainty than ever before?

Thankfully, we are not left in the dark to wonder about this question. The Apostle John wrote a letter contained in the Bible that speaks quite clearly about his knowledge of God gained by looking into the face of Christ. In his first epistle John lets it be known that one characteristic of God was now clear to him. Having seen and heard and fellowshiped with Christ, John knew this: God is love!

John's first epistle is full of this truth about God's nature. In several passages and in various ways he makes this point crystal clear.

> *How great is the love the Father has lavished on us, that we should be called children of God! (3:1)*

> *This is how we know what love is: Jesus Christ laid down his life for us. (3:16)*

> *Dear friends, let us love one another, for love comes from God. Everyone who loves has been born of God and knows God. Whoever does not love does not know God, because God is love. This is how God showed his love among us: He sent his one and only Son into the world that we might live through him. This is love: not that we loved God, but that he loved us and sent his Son as an atoning sacrifice for our sins. (4:7-10)*

> *God is love. Whoever lives in love lives in God, and God in him. (4:16)*

> *We love because he first loved us. (4:19)*

In Jesus, John discovered the matchless love of God. It was a love unlike anything a person can experience apart from Him. There are not enough descriptive words to explain the height, depth, length, and breadth of God's love. To all the broken and abused, ensnared and confused, it is *the* love that can bring freedom, healing, and meaning to life. For those afraid to approach God in the hour of need, they need only look to Jesus. There they will discover the God of love, reaching out to transform their lives.

As I have previously discussed, great fear gripped me during my "wilderness" experience. It hit with a power never before experienced and from every possible direction. As I cried out in prayer, the Lord brought to mind John's teaching that "perfect love drives out fear" (1 John 4:18). Laying hold of this truth I set out to survey Scripture, studying about God's love. I reviewed every reference to love, believing it would help me in this intense battle. What I discovered regarding the love of God was astounding. And, it certainly silenced the lies of Satan that created any unbiblical caricatures of the heavenly Father.

After this study I recorded what I discovered in my journal, and want to share it here. According to Scripture, the following words and phrases tell us either what God's love is or how His love is demonstrated:

**From Old Testament passages:**

| | |
|---|---|
| compassionate | ever increasing |
| gracious | enduring forever |
| abundant | unfailing |
| patient | a shield |
| faithful | able to save |
| forgiving | able to strengthen |
| able to deliver | faithful to remember us |
| ever before us | good |
| all about us | abounding |
| our protection | great |
| able to redeem | never ending |
| merciful | satisfying |

supportive                 able to preserve life
comforting

**From New Testament passages:**
sent His Son               gives us the kingdom
poured into us             lavished upon us
works good                 drives out fear
has chosen us              brings discipline
establishes us             preserves us to eternal life
increases our faith        causes love to abound in us
is demonstrated while
  we are yet sinners

When John wrote that God's love has been lavished upon us, he was not kidding! And it is God's great love that offers healing to all people! Far from running from God as though He were an ogre, let us run to Him through Christ! God is love!

## What Does Jesus Teach Regarding the Love of God?

It would take a complete volume to adequately illustrate the love of God displayed in the life of Jesus. However, I would like to briefly discuss four characteristics of Christ's love which I believe are most helpful to those seeking inner healing. Remember, while we see this love in the life of the Lord, it is a representation of God's love. For as we have already learned, to look into the face of Christ is to see God, for Jesus is the exact representation of His being.

## God's Love Is Unconditional and Self-Giving

Countless people today are living dysfunctional lives because they experienced distorted love. You or someone you know may be the victim of such love. It is the warped love that manipulates, demands performance, sets conditions, seeks its own gain. Twisted love gives birth to abuse, sexual molestation, people pleasing, and countless other distortions. It is impatient, harsh, selfish, inconsistent, and ultimately unfaithful. Children and adults hungry for love are seductively lured into situations and relationships that promise affection and caring, only to be abused and violated by a love that promises to give but only takes.

But God's love is perfect and in Jesus it has been expressed as unconditional and totally self-giving. The Bible tells us that God so loved the world that He gave His Son to redeem people everywhere (John 3:16). Long before you and I ever gave a thought about God, He sent Jesus to die on the cross. There He paid the penalty of our sinfulness, defeated the evil one bent on our destruction, and secured for all who believe an entirely new identity.

In Philippians 2, Paul wrote that Jesus, who is God, set aside His glory, taking on the form of a human being in order to rescue and heal us. The King of glory came to earth, born in poverty, not to get something from us, but rather to give. He came to serve, not to be served (Matthew 20:28). He came to bear our griefs, our sorrows, and our sins, not to abuse and condemn us.

God did not say, "Clean up your act, perform properly, and I will save you." Rather, while we were

yet broken, He sent Christ to set us free (Romans 5:8)!
And so, to all the broken, battered, bruised, and
abused, God says, "I give Myself to you!" But why,
you may ask? To meet your deepest needs, heal your
greatest hurts, and set you free from your strongest
chains. And He does this because He loves You!

### God's Love Is Full of Compassion

By examining the life of Jesus we see that God's love
is also expressed in deep compassion. Remember,
there is nothing that you have experienced—no hurt
or violation—that Jesus did not also experience. As a
child, He knew the sting of shame as ignorant people
whispered of His "illegitimate" birth. All throughout
His life He knew abuse, beginning with Herod's
desperate attempt to kill Him as a child, and ending
with an angry crowd shouting, "Crucify Him!" Jesus
knew rejection, cast off by the very people He came
to save. He also was pressed by thousands of people
to perform, to meet their expectations of the long-
awaited Messiah. And He was a victim of sexual
violation as He was stripped naked and nailed to the
cross. His genitals were exposed before the world as
part of the hideous practice of crucifixion.

Because Jesus felt the pain of abuse and violation He
understands our pain and moves toward us with
great love and compassion. Having shared in our
humanity, Jesus is able to sympathize with our weaknesses (Hebrews 4:15). And, out of love, He longs to
intercede for the broken, calling out, "Place your
burden on me" (see 1 Peter 5:7).

Look into the face of Jesus, and you will find a God

full of love and compassion. He is not sitting in glory, anxious to pour down coals of fire on the lost. Rather, God has reached out to us in Jesus, who knows our pain. And He continues to reach out in love to apply the oil of healing to the wounds of our pasts.

**God's Love Is Full of Mercy**

As we continue to discover the quality of God's love as seen in the face of Jesus we soon recognize that it is a most merciful love. Mercy is simply defined as not getting the punishment that a person truly deserves. Read the Gospels and one quickly sees that Jesus continually extends mercy to the undeserving.

Examples of the Lord's mercy abound. Consider the woman at the well—married five times, living with a sixth man, she surely deserved punishment. But instead Jesus extended the love of God, offering her living water that would satisfy the aching of her soul. Zacchaeus ripped off his own countrymen, filling his pockets with their money. He sold his patriotism and loyalty, exploiting the Jews on behalf of an oppressive Roman government. His own people despised him, and justifiably so. He was a traitor. But Jesus came and fully accepted him. He extended love with mercy, and it transformed Zacchaeus.

Then of course there is the woman caught in adultery. She was brutally dragged before Jesus by an angry mob ready to kill her. And according to the law, that is precisely what she deserved—death. But what did Jesus do? Out of love, He extended mercy! Instead of condemnation Jesus offered forgiveness and the challenge to "go and sin no more." Though she came to Jesus with the ugliness of her sin in full view, she left transformed by His love.

All through the Gospels we read of the Lord's encounter with the broken, rebellious, rejected, and oppressed. There was Mary Magdalene, the Gadarene, the adulterous woman who washed His feet, the countless tax collectors, sinners, and even those who crucified Him. Not one received the punishment they deserved. Touched by Jesus, they were forgiven, delivered, healed, and set free.

Satan works hard to have us believe that turning to God for help would be disastrous. But the truth is that only those who fail to turn to God ever experience punishment. Jesus clearly shows us that God is love. And His love is full of mercy. We can come before Him with all our wounds, sins, and dysfunctions. And when we do in total honesty and vulnerability, God receives us mercifully and with great compassion.

### God's Love Is Full of Grace

Finally, Jesus shows us that God's love is a most gracious love! If mercy is not receiving what we deserve, grace is being given what we could never earn or deserve! In Ephesians 2, Paul writes, "For it is by grace you have been saved, through faith—and this not from yourselves, it is the gift of God—not by works, so that no one can boast" (2:8-9). He describes the riches of God's grace as both incomparable and unsearchable. Words are inadequate to completely describe the countless gifts God lovingly bestows upon all who believe.

At the risk of dating myself, I'll point to Cecil B.

DeMille's production of *The Ten Commandments* as illustrative of the riches of salvation. Early in the movie Moses, still prince of Egypt, stands before Pharaoh to present him with gifts from Ethiopia. Scores of Ethiopians bow before Pharaoh, presenting jewels, gold, silver, priceless cloth, animals, furs, bright feathers, and rare pieces of wood. Moses then hands an account ledger to Pharaoh stating that numerous barges filled with such goods were traveling down the Nile as gifts to him. Pharaoh is overwhelmed by his prize. A prize I might add he did nothing to earn. His position alone was his right to such gifts.

The Bible says that once a person accepts Christ he or she is given a new position in His eternal kingdom. Seated with Christ, the believer is graciously put in a place to receive all the benefits of salvation. These gifts are inexhaustible, including righteousness, justification, adoption, spiritual gifts, the Holy Spirit, divine power, forgiveness of sin, healing, eternal life, heaven, wisdom, understanding, and innumerable other scriptural blessings. Paul calls these "the riches of his glorious inheritance" (1:18). All the barges in the world could not contain the inheritance promised to those who believe!

The gifts of God's gracious love are so great one could never fully know or embrace them in his or her lifetime. And to re-emphasize the critical point, each gift is given by the grace of God. No one could ever earn or deserve even the smallest part of salvation. It comes in its fullness by grace, received through faith by the lost and broken of this world. Jesus Christ paid the price, believers receive the gifts of redemption.

What greater love has the world ever seen than that displayed by Jesus? His love is unconditional and freely given. It is full of compassion and mercy. And to all who receive Him, His love brings blessings untold.

Another call just came in for me. A young woman, living with the shame of sexual infidelity, is falling apart. She is afraid, embarrassed, full of guilt, and convinced that if people ever find out she will be rejected. As we talked she described feelings of depression and a growing sense of hopelessness. Her request was simply, "May I schedule an appointment to see you? I need help."

What will I do or say when she comes? I anticipate there is more to the story than I know. And, it will most likely take several sessions to gain her trust, to lay a foundation for healing. I can predict that there are going to be some painful moments for her along the way. And there may even be strongholds of the evil one harassing her mind.

Yet I already know the ultimate prescription for her affliction—an encounter with the love of God through the person and work of Jesus Christ! I confidently turn to Him, "who is able to do immeasurably more than all we ask or imagine, according to his power that is at work within us" (3:20). Jesus, who is the full reflection of God's being, is the Gift of healing to all who hurt, whether physically, mentally, emotionally, or spiritually. His love is the power that sets the captives free!

*Chapter Ten*

# The Bondage Is Broken,
# But Beware!

*A*ndy Comiskey is a pastor and counselor with the Vineyard Christian Fellowship. He is an anointed servant of the Lord, with a powerful and effective ministry to people seeking deliverance from the homosexual lifestyle. Andy is founder and director of Desert Stream Ministry, aimed at helping the sexually dysfunctional find freedom in Jesus Christ. His book, *Pursuing Sexual Wholeness: How Jesus Heals the Homosexual*, has been a powerful instrument of healing to many people struggling with sexual confusion and disorientation.

Andy, who is both a husband and father, is a much-sought-after speaker and teacher. Certainly, the centerpiece of his ministry is the person and work of

Jesus Christ. I have heard him repeatedly state that Jesus is God's justice for the sexually broken. Andy knows that all healing, regardless of the hurt or addiction, comes through the work of our Lord. And he is quick to give Him all glory and honor for the great effectiveness of Desert Stream Ministries.

There is another reason why Andy Comiskey's ministry is so powerful. Andy, by his own testimony, bears witness to God's ability to heal those suffering from sexual dysfunction. You see, Andy met Jesus while caught in the bondage of the gay lifestyle. The Lord pressed in, bringing Andy to the place of brokenness and repentance that serves as the grand prelude to freedom. Over several years the Lord revealed to Andy the hidden inner wounds that gave birth to his sin. And by the powerful work of the Holy Spirit, God took him through the various stages of inner healing—stages that included both identification of woundings and the renunciation of demonic deceptions aimed at his self-image and true identity.

As God aligned Andy's life according to the work of Jesus, He placed within him a growing sense of emotional and spiritual wholeness. God deepened Andy's healing through marriage and the responsibilities of raising their four children.[1]

When Andy gives his testimony, people listen. I myself sat under his powerful ministry when he lectured at a healing conference in 1992. Andy's love for Christ, the anointing of the Holy Spirit, and his clear

---

[1] Andy Comiskey, "Jesus: The Father's Justice for the Sexually Broken," *Equipping the Saints*, Fall 1992, pp. 17-19.

vulnerability opened people to the Lord's healing as never before. Many caught in the devastating and destructive bondage of brokenness received guidance from one who had been there. And what they heard brought hope, for they saw in Andy a man set free by the Lord.

Andy Comiskey paints no easy, "one-two-three steps and you're free" scenario. He is honest about the depth of pain, the power of the evil one, the long season of healing, and the call to obedience. But with unmistakable joy and confidence he declares righteousness and justice to all the oppressed by the healing hand of the Lord Jesus.

As I have heard, read, and retold Andy Comiskey's testimony, my own confidence in the unsearchable riches of Christ grows. While our wounds and dysfunctions were different, the Healer is the same. And the basic pathway to inner wholeness is quite similar. First there is the recognition of sin and admission of brokenness, followed by godly sorrow that leads to repentance. Realizing one is powerless to change, the door is opened to the only One who can bring transformation. From here the season of recovery begins. Wounds are brought into the light for healing and distortions replaced by the truth of God's living Word. What eventually results is freedom and the fruits of righteousness.

My thoughts turn once again to Paul's teaching in Second Corinthians, where he wrote:

> *Now the Lord is the Spirit, and where the Spirit of the Lord is, there is freedom. And we . . . are being*

*transformed into his likeness with ever-increasing glory. (3:17-18)*

It is impossible to over-emphasize the importance of this text relative to inner healing. To all the despairing, depressed, dysfunctional, compulsive, addicted, and ensnared, it promises freedom! That freedom comes through Jesus Christ, given to all who receive Him as Savior and Lord. Indwelt by the Holy Spirit, the believer receives a completely new identity in the Lord and a salvation that is unfathomable! And if the wounded person is willing to submit to the season of healing, the Holy Spirit will use various means of grace to transform that broken soul into the likeness of Christ. This transformation goes deep, sets the captive free, and continues throughout the believer's lifetime. And to paraphrase the words of Paul in verse 18, "it keeps getting better and better" through the Lord Jesus and to His glory.

To you or someone you know suffering in the clutches of dysfunctional behavior, I declare there is hope! There is more than hope. In and through Jesus Christ there is healing. Andy Comiskey has experienced it. I am experiencing it. Scores of other men and women are now free because of Jesus. There are so many walking in new freedom that to list just those I know would turn this book into a directory. This includes people once caught in the chains of sexual addiction, chemical abuse, workaholism, people pleasing, depression, anger, rage, and fear. No wound is too severe for the Great Physician, no chain too strong for the Deliverer, no life too hopeless for the

Redeemer. Jesus has, is, and will continue to set the captives free! The bondage can be broken!

## But Beware!

As you consider and even rejoice in the freedom Christ provides for the emotionally broken, recognize this fact: while the bondage in your life can be broken, the battle may very well continue. A person can be genuinely healed and free, no longer controlled by past wounds or strongholds of the evil one. But that does not mean that trial, temptation, and deception will no longer occur. Old behaviors, direct assaults from the evil one, and the distorted standards of our society will always be there to trip us up.

While the Apostle Paul declared his own freedom in Christ, he also admitted that at times the battle was severe. In Second Corinthians 4:7-9 Paul tells believers that there were periods when he and his followers were hard pressed from every side, perplexed, persecuted, and even struck down. He, better than any theologian in history, knew what it meant to be in Christ. Our understanding of the believer's true identity and authority comes from his inspired pen. Even so, the battle continued for Paul—and be assured it will for us also.

Andy Comiskey, healed and set free by the blood of Jesus, knows that the battle continues long after the bondage is broken. Writing in *Equipping the Saints* magazine, he speaks with absolute openness about the subtle but devastating power of deception and the compassion of the Good Shepherd of the sheep:

One night after a long day of ministry, I suc-
cumbed to sexual fantasy and masturbation. I
was tired, away from home and primed for
deception. Regardless of the circumstances, I
sinned. Alone and under enemy accusation, all
I could do was cry out for mercy. I called a
friend and confessed my sin. Then I fell at
Jesus' feet and worshipped him. As I did, the
Holy Spirit deepened the conviction of my sin,
and I cried out to him from a deeper place.
Through the eyes of my heart, I witnessed the
blood and water that flowed out of Jesus' side
at his crucifixion (John 19:34) flowing right
into me. The blood washed away my sin and
the water refreshed me deep within. Having
cleansed me, his peace overpowered me as I
continued to receive from him. I inhaled the
breath of his resurrection life (John 20:21-22).
That power remains in me and frees me to
stand in my real self to this day. Satan's attempt
at a set back became an encounter with divine
grace.[2]

Once again God used Andy Comiskey to help
people who have experienced healing but are still in
the battle. Andy's blatant honesty reminds us all of
Satan's design to bring bondage back to areas Christ
has healed. The evil one hits when we are most vulnerable, where we are most susceptible and at times

---

[2]Comiskey, p. 17.

when accountability is least present. These are lessons every Christian must learn.

But we also see in Andy's testimony the work of the Holy Spirit who calls us back to our true identity in Christ. His conviction is not an instrument of punishment. Rather it is a means of discipline, correction, and realignment. The Spirit takes us back to the moment of our healing—the cross. There He renews and refreshes the repentant, bringing cleansing, peace, and the breath of life. By God's grace and through the ministry of Christ, all who slip and fall are able to claim yet again their blood-bought freedom and grace-given identity.

Regardless of the wounds, dysfunctional behaviors, symptoms of emotional upheaval, instruments of healing, or season of recovery, there are certain critical issues one must address as he or she moves from bondage to freedom. They help establish Christ's healing in the depth of our being and guard against both stumbling blocks along the pathway of peace and the tendency to feel defeated if and when one does fall.

I want to address these under the following headings:

> While the bondage is broken, what causes people to fall back into old patterns of dysfunctional behavior?

> What provision has God made to enable people to walk in wholeness and freedom?

What should a person do if in fact he or she does fall along the way?

## What Causes People to Fall Back into Old Patterns of Behavior?

I believe, by examining my life and those people I have counseled, that there are stumbling blocks before us on the road to recovery. Even though inner healing, deliverance, and freedom have been graciously given of God, these pitfalls are ever present. They must be recognized and pro-actively addressed in order to avoid their destructive and often devastating affects.

First, while healing may have come to the inner being, habits of dysfunctional behavior often remain. For years, deep wounds and deception cause a person to react inappropriately. They have done so for such a long time that it becomes a subconscious and automatic response. When placed in circumstances that previously caused problems, it is quite natural to act as one usually would. This happens even though the wounding that originally gave birth to the inappropriate behavior has been healed in Christ.

Take Jerry for example. He is a colleague who was rejected by his father during childhood and adolescence. In addition, Jerry grew up with dyslexia, a recognized learning disability. The father-wounds he carried and the repeated academic "failures" left Jerry with an incredibly low self-esteem. He lived for people's approval and acceptance. Conversely, he was paralyzed whenever anyone criticized him. Even if the critique was well-founded and constructive, it left Jerry reeling. He invariably interpreted evaluation as a personal attack.

In staff meetings Jerry would quickly defend and justify his decisions or behavior. Afterwards, he would struggle with deep and disproportionate feelings of inferiority and rejection. Other members of the staff were quick to pick up on this and, not wanting to hurt Jerry, would either preface critique with exaggerated statements of affirmation or avoid the issue and remain silent.

As with all of us, God loves Jerry and wanted to bring wholeness to the wounds that produced his people-pleasing and approval addiction. His senior pastor finally approached Jerry about his need for inner healing. Over a period of time, through a variety of instruments, the Holy Spirit worked deep within his life. The Lord revealed and touched the wounds of a childhood and adolescence that paralyzed Jerry. And God genuinely set Jerry free from the stronghold of Satan that brought feelings of inferiority. After one session Jerry said, "I finally realize I am not dumb. I am God's child."

Jerry gave testimony to God's work in his life, claiming his new freedom and identity. But he also admitted that it was still hard to receive criticism. For years Jerry interpreted it inappropriately. He had to learn new patterns of response and behavior. Quite literally he had to say to himself, "They are not attacking me or calling me a failure. My identity is in Jesus Christ and He is well pleased. If something I am doing or not doing is jeopardizing my ministry, I want to know." Jerry also chose to listen rather than justify and defend. After meetings he refused to run, but rather thanked those who offered helpful suggestions.

These behavioral changes did not come easily, because habits are strong. But by persistently renewing his mind with truth and receiving help from a counselor, Jerry was able to recognize the pitfalls of old behaviors. Occasionally he slipped and fell. But his entire way of relating was transformed.

There are countless dysfunctional behaviors that result from emotional wounds. Like ruts in a well-traveled country road, these habits are difficult to break free of, even after inner healing occurs. People need to fill in the ruts by learning appropriate responses based on truth. This truth comes from God's Word and well-balanced therapeutic behavioral training.

Long after my own healing I continued to see a therapist. I did this to recognize any and all destructive responses I habitually made in certain circumstances. I also wanted to learn new ways of relating that would compliment my emotional wholeness. Old habits can trip up any person on the path of recovery. That's why time must be invested in identifying and renouncing the old, while retraining and rehearsing new behaviors.

There is a second factor that causes people to fall back into dysfunctional behavior. It is the environment in which we live. All sections and strata of our society bombard us with deceptions that feed dysfunction. Society's values and morals are based, not on God's Word, but on the lies of the evil one.

Institutions and businesses are performance-based,

rewarding those who sacrifice all for "the cause," with little or no concern for personal well-being. I was recently listening to an interview when a young actress said, "I love New York City. Here you are accepted for what you can do, not who you are." In other words, if you perform well, you are something or somebody. What if you can't perform?

Such lies do not just come from organizations and businesses. People all around us send the same messages. Trapped in Satan's lies, they serve unknowingly as instruments of deception. As we already know, some parents demand performance, schools contribute to approval addictions, peers seek to manipulate behavior by shame and rejection. Coaches go too far when athletes make a mistake, wounding adolescents with words that make them feel like total failures. Groups isolate certain people because of the way they look, or their social class, or their race. Such actions feed feelings of rejection, deeply wound, and lead to serious emotional problems. Unchecked and unaddressed, coping mechanisms are born that sooner or later hold people in the chains of bondage.

Even as I have been writing this book I was warned, "Don't be too vulnerable; it could ruin your ministry." Such attitudes, even from Christian leaders, are based in the lie that it is better to hide than admit weakness. It is just such deceptions that keep God's servants in denial about their problems. And then, when it is far too late for salvage, their brokenness leads to disqualification.

The person in recovery must make a conscious decision to say "no" to the lies of this world's value system. He or she must pray for discernment, asking God to give the spirit of wisdom and revelation (Ephesians 1:17). Defensively, people in recovery should school themselves in society's subtle ways of shaming, guilt motivation, performance expectations, the pressure to hide, and the like. As God gives insight to recognize these deceptions, believers must say "no" in the power of Christ. If necessary, one should read about dysfunctional behavior and when possible get professional help developing "eyes" for distortion. Upon seeing it, just say NO!

Offensively, as has been stated repeatedly, people in recovery must be grounded in the truth. Repeatedly believers should renew their minds by speaking forth the reality of their new identity in Christ. In the face of society's warped value system Christians must declare, "My identity is not based upon performance. I do not *need* approval to feel worth. I am not a failure and am able to change. All of this and more is true because I have new life in Jesus Christ! He has transformed me!"

A third and most powerful source of stumbling blocks are direct assaults from the evil one and his demonic hordes. Admittedly there are diverging opinions as to the role demons play in the lives of Christians. Equally there are some disagreements regarding levels of potential demonization and procedures of deliverance. As mentioned earlier this volume is not meant to extensively address those issues. Previously I referred to several balanced and introductory works on the topic, and once again offer them as suggestions for more thorough examination.

The primary concern for most Christian leaders is one of imbalance. Some believers, including therapists and counselors, ignore this dimension of reality, acting as if demons are nonexistent. Such a position, while consistent with a humanistic world view, does not reflect the teachings of Scripture.

The Bible clearly teaches that there exists "the material world" we can see, "the transcendent world" containing God's heavenly throne, and "the spiritual world" active all around us. It is in the latter world that the angels of God and demons operate. While we cannot see this spiritual realm by human vision, it has a great effect upon our lives.

Conversely, there are many believers that emphasize demons to a fault, making them the root problem of all maladies. Such Christians spend virtually every waking hour chasing away evil spirits. In these circles more time is spent praying against Satan than glorifying God. If someone comes down with a common cold, deliverance is prescribed. Seeing demons behind every bush, such people are consumed with deliverance conferences, tapes, and books on the topic. But this too does not reflect a biblical world view. Jesus did not treat everything as a demonic problem. Some issues were rooted in simple disobedience, others illnesses and injuries, and then in several cases, demonization.

And so, a balanced Christian position reflects belief in the spiritual world around us. It also recognizes that demonic harassment, affliction, and control can be part of a person's problems, be they physical or emotional. As such, believers are commanded by

Scripture to be prepared for such attacks, fighting the forces of darkness in the power of Christ.

There have been times during my own recovery when I knew the source of a conflict was demonic. For example, on one occasion while home alone I was suddenly overcome with deep discouragement and despair. What was unusual was the fact that I had been feeling quite well, at peace, and energetic. But, without notice a most oppressive mood came over me. My mind was filled with suggestions of God's abandonment and impending judgment. I knew I was not getting "sick" again, but rather facing a pitfall. The source was not old behaviors or the value system of this world—it was in fact demonic. As I followed a scriptural approach to spiritual warfare, the Lord brought freedom and restoration as quickly as the oppression had set in upon me.

For our limited discussion, let's turn again to Ephesians 6:10-18 and embrace Paul's strategy for combating the enemy. In verse 10 he offers a command. Believers are to "be strong in the Lord and in his mighty power." He informs Christians that their own power is insufficient. Rather, believers must take their position with Christ, who has defeated the forces of Satan (2:6).

Paul reveals the reason for this admonition in verse 12. Our struggle includes battles against the "dark world" and "spiritual forces of evil." In other words, Christians are at times attacked by evil spirits. Not just sinful believers, but all believers face this battle. And only by the blood of Christ and power of His victory can Christians stand. But, praise the Lord, His power indwells us, making every Christian capable of overcoming the evil one (Romans 8:37; 1 John 4:4).

Paul then instructs Christians to do three things regularly to stand against Satan, avoiding his pitfalls. We discussed his admonitions previously in the chapter on prayer and inner healing.

First, he commands us to put on the full armor of God. For Paul to use the metaphor of armor suggests fierce battle and thus must be taken seriously. Each piece of armor represents some truth related to the finished work of Christ on our behalf. Putting on God's armor involves declaration of the Lord's victory over Satan and our identity with Him.

Secondly, as mentioned previously, we are to "pray in the Spirit on all occasions with all kinds of prayers" (Ephesians 6:18). I would encourage believers to consider one particular type of prayer as powerful against the evil one. That is the prayer of praise. Repeatedly Scripture affirms the empowerment of the believer through praise. In the Old Testament it was used as a weapon of warfare by the Israelites when facing pagan armies (2 Chronicles 20). The psalmist links praise with spiritual warfare, praying that God's people would praise God and carry a double-edged sword against their enemies (Psalm 149:6-7). As the evil one places pitfalls in our paths and launches his assaults, let us take our stand in Christ and praise His holy name!

Thirdly, Paul urges Christians to be alert. Like good soldiers, believers must be quick to recognize the enemy and his strategies to deceive or destroy.

The late David Watson, in his helpful book *How to*

*Win the War*, suggests several ways Satan seeks to attack and gain ground. The evil one comes as:

> *The Invisible Man*: Convincing people he does not exist, leaving believers powerless because they fail to fight.
>
> *The Angel of Light*: Subtly using false teachings from deceitful servants who claim to stand for righteousness but lead people astray.
>
> *The Father of Lies*: Bombarding our minds with information that is in direct opposition to the truth of Scripture.
>
> *The Accuser*: He slanders and accuses believers by pointing to past sin, and attempting to convince them that there is no hope for their deliverance.
>
> *The Roaring Lion*: He comes at times with powerful attacks, seeking to devour through fear, doubt, anger, depression or illness.
>
> *The Prince of the Power of the Air*: He commands an army of evil spirits assigned to attack Christians and the work of the Church. Most often spirits aim at weaknesses and unfortified areas in the believer's life.[3]

And so, while freedom does come, the battle continues. All Christians, particularly those in recovery, must learn to recognize and avoid the pitfalls of habits and this world system. Equally, they must be

---

[3] David Watson, *How to Win the War* (Wheaton, IL: Harold Shaw, 1972), pp. 72-78.

equipped to fight in the power of Christ. The destroyer is quick to make the most of every opportunity. Therefore we must be armed, constant in prayer, and keenly alert.

## God's Provision to Keep Us from Falling

Identifying potential pitfalls and stumbling blocks is one key step toward ongoing freedom and transformation. But in addition, believers must learn and practice God's positive prescription for good health. According to Paul, that involves carrying with us the person and work of Jesus Christ (2 Corinthians 4:10-12).

More plainly spoken, believers must focus upon the Lord Jesus Christ. According to Hebrews 3:1 and 12:1 this means concentrating one's thoughts and eyes on Jesus. Staying free demands minds consumed with His truth and eyes fixed ever upon Him. In reviewing Scripture I find it both helpful and practical to hide in our hearts: (a) what Christ has done for us; (b) what He is continuing to do on our behalf; and (c) what He places at our disposal at all times. Knowing these three aspects of our Lord's work keeps one's mind clear and vision focused. Filled with Him, there is little room then for the lies and distortions of the evil one.

### What Christ Has Done for Us

The Bible teaches that Jesus has provided all that is needed for life and godliness. Christians are able to receive inner healing, walk in freedom, and experience ongoing transformation. Fix your thoughts and eyes on these facts. Jesus has:

- Forgiven all your sins (Colossians 1:14).
- Justified you by God's grace (Romans 5:1).
- Made you righteous (2 Corinthians 5:21).
- Made you a new creation (5:17).
- Delivered you from Satan's domain (Colossians 1:13).
- Grafted you into Himself (John 15:1-5).
- Made you God's child (1:12).
- Seated you with Himself (Ephesians 2:6).
- Sealed you with the Holy Spirit (1:13-14).
- Given you access to God (Hebrews 10:19-21).
- Welcomed you into God's household (Ephesians 2:19).
- Presented heaven as your future home (Philippians 3:20).
- Provided you with eternal life (John 3:16).
- Empowered you to walk in truth (15:26; 16:12-13).
- Equipped you with spiritual gifts (1 Corinthians 12).
- Promised to be with you always (Matthew 28:20).
- Given you full membership into His body (1 Corinthians 12:27).
- Pronounced you a chosen person, royal priest, and member of His holy nation (1 Peter 2:9).

In truth, this is but a sampling of all that Christ has done for those who believe. What a glorious new identity full of gifts and promises. Fixing one's eyes and thoughts on the work of Jesus empowers any believer to take captive the lies of Satan and every pretension of evil that seeks to steal his or her blood-bought and grace-endowed inheritance.

## What Is Christ Doing for Us?

Through His death and resurrection the Lord provided a glorious inheritance for all who believe. But His ministry to Christians did not end upon His ascension. Scripture gives testimony to our Lord's ongoing intervention into the day-to-day affairs of life. Consider Hebrews 7:23-25. The author writes:

> *Now there have been many of those priests, since death prevented them from continuing in office; but because Jesus lives forever, he has a permanent priesthood. Therefore he is able to save completely those who come to God through him, because he always lives to intercede for them.*

Scripture teaches that Jesus is able to save completely those who come to God through Him. Jesus constantly serves as a bridge between believers and the heavenly Father. And according to this passage, the Lord lives to intercede for us. Jesus, the Lord of glory, continues from heaven to work on behalf of God's own. To intercede for another means to plead their case, to speak on their behalf. Jesus faithfully does this for the saved. The very thought brought me great comfort when the battle seemed too much to bear. I would imagine the Lord petitioning the Father on my behalf. In every circumstance, trial, and temptation, I could place my faith in this promised ministry of Christ Jesus. It brought and continues to bring tremendous hope and strength.

Richard Foster, referring to this ongoing ministry of the Lord writes:

> He straightens out and cleanses our feeble, misguided intercessions and makes them acceptable before a holy God. Even more still: his prayers sustain our desires to pray, urging us on and giving us hope of being heard. The sight of Jesus in his heavenly intercession gives us strength to pray in his name.[4]

Another ongoing ministry of Christ is recorded in the first epistle of John. There, the author refers to Jesus as the Advocate, who constantly speaks on behalf of Christians before the Father. An advocate is one who represents the rights and interests of another before an authority. In this case it is Jesus representing our rights before God the Father.

Satan is bent on defaming the glory of God. One attempt at this is by accusing believers of sin before the Father. He is quick to point out where we fall short, blaming believers for infidelity to God. But we need not fear his prosecution. Jesus Christ represents us as our defense Lawyer. As accusations are made and cases are presented bent on invoking God's wrath, Jesus steps in to defend. He reminds the Father that we have been redeemed by grace through faith. All sins have been paid for and debts covered by the

---

[4] Richard Foster, *Prayer: Finding the Heart's True Home* (San Francisco: Harper San Francisco, 1992), p. 193.

blood of Christ. Jesus stands to represent the believer's full rights and privileges as a child of God.

## What Jesus Christ Provides for Us

When I returned from treatment, my health was greatly improved, but I was far from completely healed. Still, it was necessary that I go back to work on a limited schedule, which included resuming my weekly preaching responsibilities. Previously I felt quite confident in this aspect of ministry. But upon my return, I found myself more anxious, somewhat fearful, and very apprehensive to preach. At the time I despised these feelings, viewing them as serious stumbling blocks to effectively proclaiming God's Word. Today I praise the Lord for my "weaknesses," for they were used of God to teach me lessons of dependence I never want to forget.

Weakness drove me to my knees like never before. There I learned the truth of the Lord's teaching to Paul in Second Corinthians:

> *"My grace is sufficient for you, for my power is made perfect in weakness." Therefore I will boast all the more gladly about my weaknesses, so that Christ's power may rest on me. . . . For when I am weak, then I am strong. (12:9-10)*

The Lord taught me to rely much more on His strength and far less upon my abilities. For years I had prayed to be a mere vessel of Christ. But there was still far too much self-confidence interfering with my Christ-confidence. But in brokenness, with self-confidence crushed, I desperately cried out to the Lord for help. He led me to several key Scriptures which taught me a new way of ministering. It is based upon the sincere confession of my inability, petitioning the Lord to help me work in His strength. Now, in all situations of ministry I pray:

- To be clothed in Christ Jesus (Romans 13:14).
- To be strengthened with power in my inner being (Ephesians 3:16).
- To receive power for every good work of faith (1 Thessalonians 1:11).
- That the name of Jesus be glorified in me (2 Thessalonians 1:12).
- That Jesus would grant me encouragement and strength (2:16-17).
- For the Lord's protection against the evil one (3:3).
- For the Lord's peace to fill my mind (3:16).
- To overflow with hope by the power of the Holy Spirit (Romans 15:13).

Weakness brings a new earnestness and urgency to such prayers. And, to the glory of Jesus Christ, I have found that He is quick to answer and faithful to empower. I believe a new effectiveness and anointing is manifest in my ministry. And it has come not out of my degrees or position or reading. It was born out of brokenness. Jesus will bring strength, hope, power, life, love, encouragement, and protection to all who genuinely cry out for help!

The key to life is not living for Jesus. Rather it is

found in Jesus living through us. This has been the testimony of countless Christians down through the ages. It is the secret we all must find. Searching for it brings an amazing discovery. The treasure has been inside of us all the time, since the day we met the Lord. Deep within each believer is the power to walk in wholeness. It is there in the person of Jesus Christ. May our hearts and minds be fixed upon Him!

## What Should We Do When We Fall?

It is, in this life, inevitable that we stumble and fall. We will sin again. We will occasionally fall back into the very dysfunctional behaviors from which we have been delivered. I have done it and surely will again. Everyone I know who has received inner healing has done likewise. Old habits are hard to break, society pressures us to conform, and the evil one is ever active to destroy. What should one do?

Let me make four suggestions. First, be quick to recognize your sin and mistake. Don't try to hide or pretend it did not happen. That only worsens the problem. In admitting, confess what you did to someone else. James tells us to confess our sins to one another for it helps the healing process (James 5:16).

Secondly, under the conviction of the Holy Spirit turn to God in repentance and sorrow. Admit what you have done, trusting in the work of Christ to provide renewal and cleansing. Confess your sin and you will find the Lord faithful and just to forgive (1 John 1:9, 2:1-2).

Thirdly, thankfully receive that cleansing. By faith trust that God has already removed the offense because of the work of Jesus Christ. Do not receive false guilt or shame, whether from other Christians, the enemy, or yourself. Guilt and shame are toxic, and if you hold on to either it can be most destructive. Also, do not punish yourself. After all, no amount of self-induced punishment can eradicate sin. Only the sacrifice of Christ is sufficient for that. Thus, if God is not punishing you, why punish yourself?

Finally, refocus on Jesus. As it says in Hebrews 12, keep your eyes on Him. It is the only way to run the race of freedom. Your thoughts fixed on Christ—what He has done, is doing and will do—is God's prescription for ongoing transformation and wholeness. Fill your mind with Jesus and learn of the unsearchable riches that are yours through Him!

In closing, I turn back to the theme of this chapter— the bondage is broken, but beware! There is healing available to the emotionally wounded, deliverance for all who are in bondage. Both come through Jesus Christ. How long it will take and what instruments He will use are up to Him. The job of the broken is to submit to Him and His process, and obey. Thankfully, Jesus provides the strength to walk through toward wholeness.

When freedom and healing come there is reason for rejoicing. It is also a time to beware. The bondage is broken, but the battle continues. This reality is no reason for discouragement or despair. The Lord has provided all one needs to walk in victory. That includes the provision to go on if and when we stumble, sin and fall back to old, destructive behaviors.

Jesus Christ truly has provided all we need for life

and godliness. In that provision is emotional healing for all who seek it in Him. And it includes the strength and power to move ahead as freedom comes.

At this point in my recovery I find particular encouragement in this passage from Second Corinthians 4. I close with this, believing it may serve you along your journey also:

> *But we have this treasure in jars of clay to show that this all-surpassing power is from God and not from us. We are hard pressed on every side, but not crushed; perplexed, but not in despair; persecuted, but not abandoned; struck down, but not destroyed. We always carry around in our body the death of Jesus, so that the life of Jesus may also be revealed in our body. (4:7-10)*

# Bibliography

## GENERAL—INNER HEALING

Anderson, Neil T. *Breaking Through to Spiritual Maturity*. Ventura, CA: Regal Books, 1992.

_____. *The Bondage Breaker*. Eugene, OR: Harvest House, 1990.

_____. *Victory Over the Darkness: Realizing the Power of Your Identity in Christ*. Ventura, CA: Regal Books, 1990.

_____. *Walking Through the Darkness*. San Bernardino, CA: Here's Life, 1991.

Backus, William. *Telling Each Other the Truth*. Minneapolis, MN: Bethany, 1985.

Backus, William, and Marie Chapman. *Telling Yourself the Truth*. Minneapolis, MN: Bethany, 1980.

Bounds, E.M. *Power Through Prayer*. Grand Rapids, MI: Baker, 1972.

Brand, Paul, and Philip Yancey. *Fearfully and Wonderfully Made*. Grand Rapids, MI: Zondervan, 1987.

_____. *In His Image*. Grand Rapids, MI: Zondervan, 1987.

Carter, Les. *Imperative People: Those Who Must Be in Control*. Nashville, TN: Thomas Nelson, 1992.

Cloud, Henry, and John Townsend. *Boundaries*. Grand Rapids, MI: Zondervan, 1992.

_____. *Changes That Heal: How to Understand Your Past to Ensure a Healthier Future*. Grand Rapids, MI: Zondervan, 1992.

_____. *When Your World Makes No Sense*. Nashville, TN: Oliver Nelson, 1990.

Dickason, C. Fred. *Demon Possession and the Christian: A New Perspective*. Wheaton, IL: Good News, 1989.

Foster, Richard. *Prayer: Finding the Heart's True Home*. San Francisco, CA: Harper San Francisco, 1992.

Garcia, Juan. *Attention Deficit Disorder*. Houston, TX: Rapha Publishing, 1991.

Greenwald, Gary L. *Seductions Exposed: The Spiritual Dynamics of Relationships*. Santa Ana, CA: Eagle's Nest Publications, 1989.

Grubb, Norman. *Rees Howells: Intercessor*. Ft. Washington, PA: Christian Literature Crusade, 1979.

Henslin, Earl. *The Way Out of the Wilderness*. Nashville, TN: Thomas Nelson, 1991.

Jacobs, Cindy. *Possessing the Gates of the Enemy*. Grand Rapids, MI: Baker/Revell, 1991.

Lawrence, Brother. *The Practice of the Presence of God*. Wilmore, KY: Christian Outreach, 1979.

MacNutt, Francis. *Healing*. New York, NY: Image Books/Doubleday, 1974.

McGee, Robert S. *Bitterness*. Houston, TX: Rapha Publishing, 1992.

_____. *The Search for Significance: Book and Workbook*. Houston, TX: Rapha Publishing, 1990.

McGee, Robert S., and Pat Springle. *Getting Unstuck*. Irving, TX: Word, 1992.

Minirth, Frank, et al. *Happiness Is a Choice*. Grand Rapids, MI: Baker, 1978.

_____. *The Path to Serenity*. Nashville, TN: Thomas Nelson, 1992.

_____. *The Thin Disguise: Understanding and Overcoming Anorexia and Bulimia*. Nashville, TN: Thomas Nelson, 1992.

Murphy, Ed. *The Handbook for Spiritual Warfare*. Nashville, TN: Thomas Nelson, 1993.

Murray, Andrew. *The Prayer Life*. Springdale, PA: Whitaker House, 1981.

Price, Richard, Pat Springle, and Joe Kloba. *Rapha's Handbook for Group Leaders* (revised edition). Houston, TX: Rapha Publishing, 1992.

Seamands, David. *Freedom from the Performance Trap*. Wheaton, IL: Victor Books, 1991.

_____. *Healing for Damaged Emotions*. Wheaton, IL: Victor Books, 1981.

_____. *Healing of Memories*. Wheaton, IL: Victor Books, 1985.

_____. *Putting Away Childish Things*. Wheaton, IL: Victor Books, 1982.

Sell, Charles. *Unfinished Business: Helping Adult Children Resolve Their Past*. Portland, OR: Multnomah, 1989.

Smalley, Gary, and John Trent. *The Blessing*. Nashville, TN: Thomas Nelson, 1986.

Spotts, Steven. *Depression*. Houston, TX: Rapha Publishing, 1991.

Stoop, David and Jan. *The Intimacy Factor: How Your Personality and Your Past Affect Your Ability to Love and Be Loved*. Nashville, TN: Thomas Nelson, 1992.

Sullivan, Barbara. *The Control Trap*. Minneapolis, MN: Bethany, 1991.

Thurman, Chris. *The Lies We Believe*. Nashville, TN: Thomas Nelson, 1989.

_____. *The Truths We Must Believe*. Nashville, TN: Thomas Nelson, 1991.

Townsend, John. *Hiding from Love: How to Change Withdrawal Patterns That Isolate and Imprison You*. Colorado Springs, CO: NavPress, 1991.

Wagner, C. Peter. *Prayer Shield: How to Intercede for Pastors, Christian Leaders and Others on the Spiritual Frontlines*. Ventura, CA: Regal, 1992.

Watson, David. *Called and Committed*. Wheaton, IL: Harold Shaw, 1982.

_____. *How to Win the War*. Wheaton, IL: Harold
Shaw, 1972.

Westmeier, Arlene. *Healing the Wounded Soul:
Ways to Inner Wholeness*. Shippensburg, PA:
Companion Press, 1991.

White, Anne S. *Freed to Live*. Winter Park, FL:
Victorious Ministry, 1989.

_____. *Healing Adventure*. Winter Park, FL:
Victorious Ministry, 1969.

_____. *Trial by Fire*. Kirkwood, MO: Impact Books,
1975.

Woititz, Janet. *Struggle for Intimacy*. Deerfield Beach,
FL: Health Communications, 1985.

_____. *Guidelines for Support Groups*. Deerfield
Beach, FL: Health Communications, 1992.

## *ANXIETY/FEAR*

Minirth, Frank, et al. *Worry Free Living*. Nashville,
TN: Thomas Nelson, 1989.

Randau, Karen. *Anxiety Attacks*. Houston, TX:
Rapha Publishing, 1991.

_____. *Conquering Fear*. Houston, TX: Rapha Publishing, 1991.

## CHEMICAL DEPENDENCY

Anonymous. *Go Ask Alice*. New York, NY: Avon, 1976. (For children with a chemical dependency).

Black, Claudia. *Repeat After Me*. Denver, CO: MAC Publishing, 1991.

Jesse, Rosalie. *Children in Recovery*. New York, NY: Norton, 1989.

McGee, Robert S. *Chemical Dependency*. Houston, TX: Rapha Publishing, 1991.

McGee, Robert S., et al. *Twelve Step Program for Overcoming Chemical Dependency*. Irving, TX: Word, 1990.

Woititz, Janet. *Adult Children of Alcoholics*. Deerfield Beach, FL: Health Communications, 1990.

For Additional Books on Alcohol/Drug Abuse:
Hazelden Catalog
15291 Pleasant Valley Road
Center City, MN 55012-0176

## CODEPENDENCY

Allender, Dan B., and Tremper Longman III. *Bold Love*. Colorado Springs, CO: NavPress, 1992.

_____. *Bold Love Discussion Guide*. Colorado Springs, CO: NavPress, 1992.

Beattie, Melody. *Beyond Codependency: And Getting Better All the Time*. New York, NY: Harper-Collins, 1989.

_____. *Codependent No More: How to Stop Controlling Others and Start Caring for Yourself*. New York, NY: HarperCollins, 1987.

Buhler, Rich. *Pain and Pretending: Discovering the Causes of Your Codependency*. Nashville, TX: Thomas Nelson, 1988.

Hemfelt, R., F. Minirth, P. Meier, and D. & B. Newman. *Love Is a Choice: Recovery for Codependent Relationships*. Nashville, TN: Thomas Nelson, 1989.

_____. *Love Is a Choice Workbook*. Nashville, TN: Thomas Nelson, 1991.

Springle, Pat. *Close Enough to Care*. Houston, TX: Rapha Publishing, 1991.

_____. *Codependency*. Houston, TX: Rapha Publishing, 1991.

_____. *Codependency: Breaking Free from the Hurt and Manipulation of Dysfunctional Relationships*. Irving, TX: Word, 1989.

_____. *Twelve Steps to Overcoming Codependency*. Irving, TX: Word, 1990.

## COMPULSIVE BEHAVIORS

Crabb, Larry. *Inside Out*. Colorado Springs, CO: NavPress, 1991.

_____. *Inside Out Study Guide*. Colorado Springs, CO: NavPress, 1992.

Hart, Archibald D. *Healing Life's Hidden Addictions*. Ann Arbor, MI: Servant Publications, 1990.

Minirth, Frank, et al. *We Are Driven*. Nashville, TN: Thomas Nelson, 1991.

## EATING DISORDERS

Banks, Bill. *Deliverance from Fat and Eating Disorders*. Kirkwood, MO: Impact Books, 1988.

Boone-O'Neill, Cherry. *Starving for Attention*. New
    York, NY: Continuum, 1982.

Hall, Lindsey, and Leigh Cohn. *Bulimia: A Guide to
    Recovery*. Carlsbad, CA: Gurze Publications,
    1989.

McGee, Robert S., and William D. Mountcastle.
    *Twelve Step Program for Overcoming Eating
    Disorders*. Irving, TX: Word, 1990.

Messinger, Lisa. *Biting the Hand That Feeds Me: Days
    of Binging, Purging, and Recovery*. Novato, CA:
    Arena Press, 1986.

Minirth, Frank, et al. *Love Hunger: Recovery from
    Food Addiction*. New York, NY: Fawcett, 1991.

Spotts, Steven. *Eating Disorders*. Houston, TX:
    Rapha Publishing, 1991.

## *FAMILY ISSUES*

Berman, W.B., D.R. Doty, and J.H. Graham. *Shaking
    the Family Tree: Use Your Family's Past to Strengthen
    Your Family's Future*. Wheaton, IL: Victor, 1991.

Carder D., E. Henslin, J. Townsend, H. Cloud, and
    A. Brawand. *Secrets of Your Family Tree*. Chicago,
    IL: Moody, 1991.

Carlson, Randy L. *Father Memories*. Chicago, IL: Moody, 1992.

Carter, Lee.Irving, *Family Communication*. TX: Word, 1992.

_____. *KidThink*. Irving, TX: Word, 1992.

Hemfelt, Robert and Paul Warren. *Kids Who Carry Our Pain: Breaking the Cycle of Codependency for the Next Generation*. Nashville, TN: Thomas Nelson, 1990.

McGee, Robert S. *Discipline with Love*. Houston, TX: Rapha Publishing, 1991.

Springle, Pat, et al. *Your Parents and You*. Irving, TX: Word, 1990.

Stoop, David. *Making Peace with Your Father*. Wheaton, IL: Tyndale, 1992.

Stoop, David, and James Masteller. *Forgiving Our Parents, Forgiving Our Selves*. Ann Arbor, MI: Servant Publications, 1991.

Van Vonderen, Jeff. *Families Where Grace Is in Place*. Minneapolis, MN: Bethany, 1992.

Wilson, Sandra. *Shame-Free Parenting*. Downer's Grove, IL: InterVarsity, 1992.

## HOMOSEXUALITY

Comiskey, Andrew. "Jesus: The Father's Justice for
the Sexually Broken." *Equipping the Saints*, Fall,
1992.

_____. *Pursuing Sexual Wholeness*. Altamonte
Springs, FL: Creation House, 1989.

Payne, Leanne. *The Broken Image*. Wheaton, IL:
Crossway Books, 1981.

_____. *Crisis in Masculinity*. Wheaton, IL:
Crossway Books, 1985.

_____. *The Healing of the Homosexual*. Wheaton,
IL: Crossway Books, 1984.

_____. *The Healing Presence*. Wheaton, IL:
Crossway Books, 1989.

Saia, Michael. *Counseling the Homosexual*. Minneapolis, MN: Bethany, 1988.


## MEN'S ISSUES

Dalbey, Gordon. *Father and Son: The Wound, the
Healing, the Call to Manhood*. Nashville, TN:
Thomas Nelson, 1992.

_____. *Healing the Masculine Soul*. Irving, TX: Word, 1991.

Jones, G. Brian, and Linda Phillips-Jones. *Men Have Feelings Too!*. Wheaton, IL: Victor Books, 1988.

McGee, Robert S. *Father Hunger*. Ann Arbor, MI: Servant Publications, 1993.

## *SEXUAL ABUSE*

Allender, Dan B. *The Wounded Heart: Hope for Adult Victims of Childhood Sexual Abuse*. Colorado Springs, CO: NavPress, 1990.

_____. *The Wounded Heart Workbook*. Colorado Springs, CO: NavPress, 1992.

Frank, Jan. *A Door of Hope: Recognizing and Resolving the Pains of Your Past*. San Bernardino, CA: Here's Life, 1987.

Heitritter, Lynn, and Jeanette Vought. *Helping Victims of Sexual Abuse*. Minneapolis, MN: Bethany, 1989.

Kubetin, Cynthia A., and James Mallory. *Beyond the Darkness*. Houston, TX: Rapha Publishing, 1992.

Mallory, James. *Sexual Abuse*. Houston, TX: Rapha Publishing, 1992.

Sandford, Paula. *Healing Victims of Sexual Abuse.*
Tulsa, OK: Victory House, Inc., 1988.

## *SHAME*

Henslin, Earl. *The Way Out of the Wilderness: Learn How Bible Heroes with Feet of Clay Are Models for Your Recovery.* Nashville, TN: Thomas Nelson, 1992.

Rainey, Russ. *Shame.* Houston, TX: Rapha Publishing, 1992.

Smedes, Lewis B. *Shame and Grace: Healing the Shame We Don't Deserve.* San Francisco, CA: Harper San Francisco, 1993.

Wilson, Sandra. *Released from Shame: Recovery for Adult Children of Dysfunctional Families.* Downer's Grove, IL: InterVarsity, 1991.

_____. *Shame-Free Parenting.* Downer's Grove, IL: InterVarsity, 1992.

## *SPIRITUAL ABUSE*

Arterburn, Stephen, and Jack Felton. *Toxic Faith: Understanding and Overcoming Religious Addiction.* Nashville, TN: Oliver Nelson, 1991.

Johnson, David, and Jeff VanVonderen. *The Subtle Power of Spiritual Abuse*. Minneapolis, MN: Bethany, 1991.

Mains, David. *Healing the Dysfunctional Church Family*. Wheaton, IL: Victor Books, 1992.

## VERBAL ABUSE

Ketterman, Grace. *Verbal Abuse: Healing the Hidden Wound*. Ann Arbor, MI: Servant Publications, 1992.

## WOMEN'S ISSUES

Norwood, Robin. *Women Who Love Too Much: When You Keep Wishing and Hoping He'll Change*. Kirkwood, NY: J.P. Tarcher (Putnam), 1985.

Sandford, Paula. *Healing Women's Emotions*. Tulsa, OK: Victory House, Inc., 1992.

Wright, Norman. *Always Daddy's Girl*. Ventura, CA: Regal Books, 1989.

# FOR THOSE IN DOUBT . . .

Collins, Gary R. *Can You Trust Psychology?*.
  Downer's Grove, IL: InterVarsity, 1988.

Hurding, Roger F. *The Tree of Healing*. Grand
  Rapids, MI: Zondervan, 1985.

Kirwan, William T. *Biblical Concepts for Christian
  Counseling: A Case for Integrating Psychology and
  Theology*. Grand Rapids, MI: Baker, 1984.

Playfair, William L. *The Useful Lie*. Wheaton, IL:
  Crossway Books, 1991.

White, John. *Putting the Soul Back in Psychology*.
  Downer's Grove, IL: InterVarsity, 1987.

If you are interested in Recovery
Training or Inner Healing,
please contact CFM


Cornerstone Formation Ministries, Inc.
259 Sandusky Street
Ashland, Ohio 44805